WOMEN IN BUDDHIST LITERATURE

WOMEN IN BUDDHIST LITERATURE

BIMALA CHURN LAW

GYAN

Published by

GYAN

Gyan Publishing House
5, Ansari Road
Daryaganj, New Delhi-110002
Phone: 011-47034999, 9811692060
E-mail: books@gyanbooks.com

Distribution Network
gyanbooks.com
India, USA, Canada, UK, Australia, France

ISBN : 978-81-212-4225-7 (PB)
First Published, Ceylon, 1927

2nd Impression 2020

Printed at: Gyan Press, Delhi.

Women in Buddhist Literature
Author: Bimala Churn Law

WOMEN IN BUDDHIST LITERATURE

BY

BIMALA CHURN LAW, Ph. D., M. A., B. L.,

Sir Asutosh Mookerjee Gold Medalist,
Calcutta University,
Corporate Member, American Oriental Society.

Author, Some Kṣatriya Tribes of Ancient India,
Ancient Mid-Indian Ksatriya Tribes,
Ancient Indian Tribes,
The Life and Work of Buddhaghosa,
Buddhist Conception of Spirits,
Heaven and Hell in Buddhist Perspective, etc., etc.

W. E. BASTIAN & Co.,

CEYLON

1927

PREFACE

The subject of women as depicted in the Pali literature is an interesting one. I have been long contemplating of writing something about this topic. I have attempted in this treatise to do justice to the subject; but how far I have succeeded, it is for the public to judge. I have made use of all original Pali books. This work is, I believe, the first of its kind.

I am grateful to Messrs. W. E. Bastian & Co. for speedy publication of this work.

24, Sukea Street,
Calcutta,
October, 1927.

BIMALA CHURN LAW.

CONTENTS

Women in Buddhist Literature

INTRODUCTION

Buddhism in spite of its catholic ideas did not at first place women on a level with men. Nevertheless women played not an inconspicuous part in the early history of Buddhism. And we quite agree with Mrs. Rhys Davids that through and in Buddhism the Indian women secured a real advance. But the advance was the work of the women themselves. "Women fought their own battle along the line all the time and forced the hand of the good but reluctant saviours of women." It was women who made men and their churches recognise them (women). It is true that the nuns by the rules of their order rank lower than monks. A nun of even a hundred years standing was to rise and respectfully salute even the youngest monk; she must submit to receive admonition from him. Further a nun may not keep vassa in a district in which no monk is resident (Cullavagga, X., I., S. B. E., XX., 323). It is probable that the ordination of women as bhikkhuṇīs and the establishment of nunneries are in reality due to a later age than that of the founder of Buddhism. The institution has never become popular or gained a strong hold in any Buddhist country and the number of the nuns has always been small relatively to the number of monks. Buddha was never tired of describing the defects and vices of women and warning the monks to guard against them. (Hastings, Encyclopædia of Religion and Ethics, V., p. 453). But it should not be ascribed merely to contempt for the weaker sex, for similar warnings are given to women as regards the wickedness of men (cf. A. N., IV., 196-197). Prof. Hopkins has recorded his views about women in his well-known work, "Ethics of India." He says that women are reviled as being "torches that light the way to hell," and even the popular teaching of the Jātakas is full of diatribes against them, not only wicked women, but, as is expressly said, "all women." The Bodhisatta himself calls a great congregation together, and he and other saints recount all the stories against women that they can remember, proving that women in general are a debauched and worthless set of beings, some of these stories being heightened by deliberate falsification of traditional material. The burden of these exhortations is that "all women go wrong if given opportunity." Nārada, a great saint, says that oceans, kings, Brāhmaṇas and women are the four insatiates. (Cf. Kunāla Jātaka, Fausböll, No. 536). At the same time, duty to parents is imperative and the "mother is the way to heaven." She must always be tenderly cared for. Moreover nuns were soon admitted into the Buddhistic Order, and though they were not allowed to be autonomous they were highly respected. The diatribes seem to be intended for monkish recluses, to guard them in the main against losing their accumulated merits by unholy imaginings. (pp. 162-163). Again we read of females in the higher ranks who never stepped upon the ground for delicateness; but when individuals are brought before us as Mahāmāyā or Visākhā we see them moving freely in general society and speaking to men without restraint. It was the custom for certain classes of women to wander about from place to place and challenge even men to enter into controversy with them apparently without any sense of impropriety on their part or of condemnation in the minds of others. These criteria are confessedly indefinite; but yet, in the absence of more authoritative demonstration, they are of some value, as they seem to fix the era of the commencement of Buddhism in some age previous to the oldest of the philosophies now received on the continent of India. (Spence Hardy, Legends and Theories of the Buddhists, pp. XXIV-XXV). Sir Charles Eliot points out that Buddhism has done nothing to support or commend the system of the harem. In some Buddhist countries such as Burma and Siam, women enjoy almost the same independence as in Europe. In China and Japan their status is not so high, but the period when Buddhism was powerful in Japan (800-1100 A. D.) was marked by a number of female writers, and among the Tibetans women enjoy considerable freedom and authority (Eliot, Hinduism and Buddhism, I. 248). Recently our attention has been drawn to an article in the Buddhist Chronicle on "Women in Buddhism" which seems to be a popular rather than a learned treatise on the subject. In the following pages we have attempted for the first time a systematic and comprehensive treatment of the subject.

CHAPTER I

MARRIAGE

In the Buddhist epoch as in other periods of Indian history the greater part of a woman's life is taken up in her marriage and marital relations. We do not find any hard and fast rule about the age at which girls are to be married, nor do we come across instances of early marriage. Girls are sometimes seen to have been married at the age of sixteen. In the Asilakkhaṇa Jātaka (No. 126) we read that a princess was given in marriage when she was sixteen years old. The Dhammapada commentary (II. 217) says that Kuṇḍalakesī, a beautiful daughter of a banker of Rājagaha, remained unmarried till the age of sixteen. It further says that at this age women long for men (tasmin ca vaye ṭhitā nāriyo purisajjhāsaya honti purisalolā).

Marriageable age of girls.

Limitations on marriage imposed by Brahmanic usage are conspicuous by their absence in Buddhist literature and even sister-marriage is referred to. The mythical origin of the Licchavis as recorded in the Paramatthadīpanī on the Khuddakapāṭha (Ed. by H. Smith, pp. 158-160) illustrates our point.

Sister-marriage.

The Sumaṅgalavilāsinī (pt. I., pp. 258-260) presents us with another instance of marriage not allowed by Brahmanic scriptures. It says that King Okkāka had five queens. By the chief queen, he had four sons and five daughters. After the death of the chief queen, the king married another young lady who extorted from him the promise to place her son upon the throne. The king thereupon requested his sons to leave the kingdom. The princes accordingly left the kingdom accompanied by their sisters, and going to a forest near the Himālayas they began to search for a site for building a city. In course of their search, they met the sage Kapila who said that they should build a town in the place where he (the sage) lived. The princes built the town and named it Kapilavatthu (Kapilavastu). In course of time, the four brothers married the four sisters, excepting the eldest one and they came to be known as the Śākyas. The Mahāvamsa also refers to sister-marriage. It says that Sīhabāhu, ruler of the kingdom of Lāḷa, made his sister Sīhasīvalī his queen.[1]

It is, however, difficult to say how far the Buddhist stories about the origin of some famous political communities by sister-marriage can be regarded as historical. Sister-marriage was not in vogue in Ancient India even in the earliest times of which we have any record, as the story of Yama and Yamī in the Ṛg-Veda amply demonstrates. The idea was revolting to the Indians from the time of the Ṛg-Veda downwards.

Marriage of a woman with her cousin.

The marriage of cousins, on the other hand, seems to have been by no means unusual. The marriage of Princess Vajirā with King Ajātaśatru, the son of her father's sister, is an illustration of this kind of marriage. Magha, a householder of Magadha, married his maternal uncle's daughter named Sujātā. (Dhammapada commentary,

1. Lāḷaraṭṭhe pure tasmin Sīhabāhu narādhipo rajjam kāresi katvāna mahesiṁ Sīhasīvalīṁ. (Mahāvaṁsa, Geiger's Ed. p. 60, cf. Ibid, Ch. VII., Sls. 67-68).

265). Ānanda was enamoured of the beauty of his father's sister's daughter named Uppalavannā and wanted to marry her. (Ibid, II, p. 49). This shows that cousins could marry. This is also borne out by the following Jātaka story (No. 262; cf. No. 126). A king had a daughter and a nephew who were in love with each other. The king intended to marry his nephew with a princess of some other country and his daughter with a prince of some other kingdom. The king guarded his daughter very closely. One night he watched his daughter and let her rest upon a little bed in his presence. She lay down without going to sleep. A little while after she said, "Father, I want to bathe". "Come along, my daughter", said the king. Holding her hands the king led her to the window; he lifted her and placed her on a lotus ornament outside it, holding her by one hand. As she bathed herself, she held out a hand to the prince, the nephew of the king and lover of the daughter. The prince loosed off the bangles from her arm, and fastened them on the arm of his soft-handed page-boy; then he lifted the lad and placed him upon the lotus beside the princess. She took his hand, and placed it in her father's and went away with the prince. The king considered the lad to be his own daughter; and when the bathing was over, he put him to sleep in the royal bed chamber, shut the door and set his seal on it; then setting a guard he returned to his own chamber and lay down to rest. The next morning he opened the door and saw the lad. The lad being questioned told the king how his daughter had fled with the prince. The king was cast down and thought, "Not even if one goes along and holds hands, can one guard a woman." Then he gave his daughter in marriage to the prince, his nephew who, on his maternal uncle's death, ascended the throne.

In the Mahāvaṁsa also we find references to cousin marriage.[1] Cittā, daughter of King Paṇḍuvāsudeva of Laṅkā, was so very beautiful that anybody seeing her would run mad. Hence Cittā was called Ummādacittā. Afraid of a prophecy that Cittā's son would kill Cittā's brothers for the throne, the princes kept their only sister in a chamber having but one pillar and the entry to the chamber lay through the king's sleeping apartment. Cittā had only one serving woman. One day she saw her maternal uncle's son named Dīghagāmani and fell in love with him at first sight. With the help of the maid, Gāmani used to get into princess' chamber stealthily every night and had intercourse with her. Matters went on in this way for sometime till Cittā was discovered to be with child. The serving woman informed the queen who, having questioned her daughter, brought the matter to the notice of the king. The king in consultation with his sons gave Cittā in marriage with her lover who was her maternal uncle's son.[2]

Suvannapālī was married and made queen by her father's sister's son named Puṇḍakābhaya.[3]

Different forms of Marriage.

Marriage was usually of three forms:—(1) Marriage arranged by guardians of both parties (2) Svayambara marriage and (3) Gandharva marriage.

---

1. Pitucchādhitaraṁ taṁ so ādāya dhajinīpeti gantvāna vaṅganagaraṁ saṁvāsaṁ tāya kappayi (Geiger's Ed. p. 58).

2. Mahāvaṁsa, Geiger's Ed., ch, IX

3. Ibid., ch. X., Sl. 78.

The common form of marriage was that arranged by guardians of both the parties and established between two families of the same caste and equal rank. This was akin to the Prājāpatya form of marriage current amongst the Hindus. Equality of birth and not of wealth was a matter of primary consideration before the settlement of a marriage. The Sāvatthian treasurer, Migāra, for instance, considered the equality of birth before he agreed to the proposal sent by treasurer Dhanañjaya of Sāketa for the marriage of his daughter, Visākhā with Migāra's son (Buddhist Parables, p. 161; cf. Dhammapada commentary Vol. I., p. 390). In the Babbu Jātaka (No. 137) we read that a Sāvatthian girl named Kāṇā was married to a husband of the same caste in another village. The Nakkhatta Jātaka (No. 49) tells us that a gentleman of the country near Sāvatthī asked in marriage for his son a young Sāvatthian lady of equal rank. We learn from the Therīgāthā commentary (p. 260) that Isidāsī, daughter of a virtuous and wealthy merchant, was married to a merchant's son of equal position. Uttarā, daughter of Nandaka, commander-in-chief of Piṅgala, king of Suraṭṭha, was married to one of a family of equal position. (P. D. on Petavatthu, pp. 244-257).

The Vimānavatthu informs us that a daughter of an upāsaka at Sāvatthī was married to a member of another family of equal status (Vimānavatthu Commentary, p. 128). The Manorathapūraṇī tells us that Sigālakamātā who came of the Treasurer's family at Rājagaha was married to a family of equal rank (p. 227).

The usual practice in the form of marriage

mentioned above was that the bridegroom used to come to the bride's house for marriage. The bridegroom and his party were received with great honour and were provided with both lodgings and requisites, garlands, perfumes, garments and the rest.

Exceptions regarding caste and rank are sometimes met with in several works such as the Viruḍhakāvadāna in the Avadānakalpalatā, the Therīgāthā, the Mahāvaṁsa and the Jātakas. Pasenadi, king of Kośala, married a slave-girl of Sākya Mahānāman and took her with him in great pomp to Srāvastī. This girl was called Mallikā well-known for her wonderful touch. Pasenadi while intending to establish a connection with the Buddha's family by marriage, was deceived by the Sākyas who gave him in marriage, a girl named Vāsabhakhattiyā, a daughter by a slave-woman of one of their leading chiefs, Mahānāman. This deception was avenged by Viḍūḍabha, son of Pasenadi by Vāsabhakhattiyā (cf. Introduction to Kaṭṭhahāri Jātaka, No. 7; Dhammapada commentary, Vol. I., pp. 345 foll). Aśoka made a merchant's daughter named Devī his wife who bore him, in course of time, a son named Mahinda and a daughter named Saṅghamittā (Mahāvaṁsa, p.101). The marriage of Kisāgotamī, daughter of a poverty-stricken house, with the son of a rich merchant was not preceded by any consideration of caste or rank. (Dhammapada commentary, II., p. 270). Similarly the equality of birth, family and wealth had to be sacrificed by the parents of Kuṇḍalakesī in marrying her with a thief with whom she fell in love at first sight from the top of her house. (Ibid., p 217). Cāpā, daughter of the chief of the hunters of Vaṅkahāra country, was given to an ascetic named Upaka as his wife. Upaka lived near the hunter's house where he used to go for alms. Once the hunter had to go out for seven days on a hunting excursion. Cāpā was asked to wait upon the ascetic. The first day the ascetic came to the hunter's house for alms, Cāpā came out and gave him alms. Upaka was captivated by her beauty. He returned home and lay fasting for seven days being fired by lust. The hunter came back and learnt everything. Thereupon he gave his daughter Cāpā to the ascetic Upaka as his bride. (Therīgāthā commentary, pp. 220 foll). The circumstances which brought about the union of the hunter's daughter with an ascetic go to show that consideration of caste or rank was sometimes sacrificed in exceptional circumstances. Cāpā, it might be said without fear of contradiction, was given by her father to an ascetic out of respect towards the latter. The story of Triśaṅku, the Caṇḍāla chieftain, narrated in the Divyāvadāna, is the only instance indicating the marriage of a brahmin daughter with the Caṇḍāla's learned son Sārdulakarṇa. (p. 620, *et. seq.*)

Svayambara.

The second form of marriage was Svayambara or a girl's publicly choosing a husband for herself from a number of suitors assembled for the purpose. The Kuṇāla Jātaka (No. 536) refers to the Svayambara marriage of princess Kaṇhā who, on seeing the five sons of King Paṇḍu, viz: Ajjuna, Nakula, Bhīmasena, Yudiṭṭhila and Sahadeva in the Svayambara assembly, fell in love with all five, threw a wreathed coil of flowers on their heads while they were standing before her, and said, "Dear mother, I choose these five men". She was allowed to have these five men as her husbands. This is evidently a reminiscence of the celebrated Svayambara marriage of Draupadī recorded in the Mahābhārata. In the Nacca Jātaka (No. 32) also we read that a princess prayed to her father for a boon that she might be allowed to choose a husband for herself. With a view to grant her prayer, the king invited all princes to a Svayambara sabhā convened for the purpose. Princes from all countries assembled there. The king sent for his daughter and bade her go and choose a husband after her own heart. The girl appeared before the assembly and selected one as her life-mate. The selected husband was then found to be wanting in modesty and was therefore disapproved by the king.

Generally do we find in the Hindu literature that a person chosen by a maid in a Svayambara assembly becomes the husband of the maid despite his demerits. Of course in such an assembly kings and princes are suitors. But this appears to be an exceptional instance in which the final verdict rests with the bride's father.

The Dhammapada Commentary furnishes us with another reference to Svayambara marriage. It tells us that Vepacitti, king of the Asuras, refused to give his daughter in marriage to any of the Asura princes. So he said, "My daughter shall choose for herself such a husband as she sees fit." He then assembled the host of Asuras, made over a garland of flowers to his daughter and said to her, "Choose for yourself a husband who suits you." The girl selected one as her husband and threw the wreath over his head. (Dhammapada commentary, Vo. I., pp. 278-279).

Gandharva Marriage.

The third form of marriage is what may be called the Gandharva form of marriage in which the bride and the bridegroom make their own choice without the knowledge of their guardians and are married without rites or ceremonies.

The Kaṭṭhahāri Jātaka (No. 7) gives us an instance of this Gandharva form of marriage. Once a king having gone in great state to his pleasure-garden was wandering hither and thither for fruits and flowers. He saw a woman who was merrily singing away as she picked up sticks in the grove. The king fell in love with her at first sight and became intimate with her. The woman knew and told the king that she would become a mother. The king gave her the signet-ring from his finger and said, "If it be a girl, spend this ring on her nurture; but if it be a boy, bring ring and child to me." In course of time a child was born. When the child could run about and play, he was taken by his mother to the king with the signet ring. After great difficulty the boy was proved to be the son of the king who made him viceroy and his mother queen-consort. This story reminds us of the well-known union of Śakuntalā with king Duṣyanta in the Abhijñāna Śakuntalaṁ of Kālidāsa.

Elopement.

Women were sometimes seduced and abducted. These eloped women were subsequently married in some cases and in others they used to pass off as wives without going through any matrimonial rite. In the Dhammapada Commentary (Vol. I., p. 191 foll) we read that Vāsuladattā, daughter of Caṇḍapajjota of Ujjain, was given by her father to Udena to teach her the manta for capturing elephants. Udena fell in love with Vāsuladattā and eloped with her. Afterwards Udena married her and made her his queen. The same work (Vol. II., p. 260 foll) informs us that Paṭācārā was the daughter of a rich banker of Sāvatthī. When sixteen she was kept on the topmost floor of a seven-storied palace and was guarded with excessive care; but she fell in love with her own page. On the day fixed for her marriage with another youth, equal in birth and rank, she eloped with her lover, took shelter in a distant village and dwelt in a hamlet. Nowhere in this account do we find that Paṭācārā was married by her paramour subsequent to elopement. But they passed off as husband and wife and in course of time Paṭācārā gave birth to a child. (cf. Therīgāthā commentary, p. 108). The Assaka Jātaka (No. 100) also says that the king of Kosala came up with a great force against the king of Benares, slew the king and bore off his queen to be his own wife. A similar instance of the abduction of a woman is met with in the Takka Jātaka (No. 63) which says that a village girl was kidnapped and kept as wife by a robber chieftain.

Seclusion of Women.

To guard against elopement, abduction and unions not sanctioned by custom, women were often kêpt inside the purdah. We learn from the Dhammapada Commentary that a rich man's daughter, when she attained marriageable age, was lodged by her parents in an apartment of royal splendour on the topmost floor of a seven-storied palace, with a female slave to guard her. No male servant was kept in that house. (Ibid., Vol. II., p. 217).

Daughters of noble families did not ordinarily come out of their house, but they travelled in chariots and the like, while others entered an ordinary carriage or raised a parasol or a palmyra-leaf over their heads; but if this was not available, they took the skirt of their undergarment and threw it over their shoulder (Dhammapada commentary, Vol. I., p. 391.) From the instances cited above it is reasonable to hold that elopement and the preservation of chastity *inter alia* contributed largely to the observance of purdah by the tender sex before or after-marriage. But there are exceptions. Visākhā, for example, while going to her father-in-law's house just after her marriage entered the city of Sāvatthī not under the purdah but standing up in a chariot uncovered showing herself to all the city. (D. C., I., p. 384 foll). Daughters of respectable families who did not ordinarily stir out, used to go on foot, during a festival, with their own retinue and bathe in the river. (Dhammapada commentary, I., pp. 190-191 and 388). These instances indeed show a relaxation of the purdah system.

Auspicious days observed for the celebration of marriage.

Lucky days were arranged for marriage in which the bride or bridegroom was brought home or sent forth (Dīgha Nikāya, Vol. I., p. 11). Marriage ceremonies were held during auspicious hours which were strictly observed by some. We learn from the Nakkhatta Jātaka that a naked ascetic was consulted as to whether stars were favourable for holding marriage ceremonies. The fixed day was found to be inauspicious and the bridegroom did not come to the bride's house for marriage. (Jātaka, No. 49).

Dowry. The Buddhist literature hardly mentions the prevalence of dowry system in connection with marriage ceremonies. But instances of dowry being given by the bride's father are referred to in the Visākhāyavatthu of the Dhammapada commentary, (Vol. 1.) The Sāvatthian treasurer, Migāra, on the occasion of the marriage of his daughter, Visākhā, well-known in the Buddhist literature, gave her as dowry five hundred carts filled with money, five hundred carts filled with vessels of gold, five hundred filled with vessels of silver, five hundred filled with copper vessels, five hundred filled with garments made of various kinds of silk, five hundred filled with ghee, five hundred filled with rice-huskėd and winnowed, and five hundred filled with plows, plowshares, and other farm implements. Sixty thousand powerful bulls and sixty thousand milchcows, and some powerful bull-calves were also given to her.

Bath and perfume money. The Dhammapada commentary and the Jātakas tell us that marriage of girls was celebrated with bath-money given by the father to his daughter. Mahā-Kosala, father of Pasenadi, king of Kosala, married his daughter Kosala-devī to King Bimbisāra of Magadha and gave her a village in Kāsī for her bath and perfume money (Jātakas, Nos. 239 & 283). Princess Vajirā was the daughter of Pasenadi of Kosala. She was given in marriage to Ajātasatru of Magadha. Kāsīgāma was given to her by her father for her bath and perfume money (Dhammapada Commentary, Vol. III., 266). The Sāvatthian treasurer, Migāra, gave his daughter, on her marriage, fifty-four crores of treasure to buy aromatic powders for the bath (Ibid., Vol. I., p. 398).

Levy on the occasion of a marriage ceremony.

The custom of collecting presents (paṇṇākāram) on the occasion of a marriage ceremony is met with in the Dhammapada commentary (Vol. I., p 182) where we read that on the occasion of the marriage ceremony of Visākhā, daughter of Dhanañjaya seṭṭhī, with the son of Migāraseṭṭhī, presents including a hundred each of all kinds of gifts were collected from hundred villages.

Admonitions to a married girl.

After marriage the girl was sent to her father-in-law's house with the following admonitions:[1]

(1) Do not carry outside the indoor fire.
(2) Do not carry inside the outdoor fire.
(3) Give only to him that gives.
(4) Do not give him that does not give.
(5) Give both to him that gives and him that does not give.
(6) Sit happily.
(7) Eat happily.
(8) Sleep happily. (9) Tend the fire.
(10) Honour the household Divinity.

These ten admonitions were interpreted as follows:—

(1) If the mother-in-law or other female members of the household engage in a private conversation within the house, their conversation is not to be communicated to slaves, whether female or male, for such conversation is tattled about and causes quarrels.

1. Antoaggi bahi na nīharitabbo, bahi aggi anto na pavesetabbo, dadantass' eva dātabbam, adadantassa na dātabbaṁ, dadantassāpi adadantassāpi dātabbaṁ, sukhaṁ nisīditabbaṁ, sukhaṁ bhuñjitabbaṁ, sukhaṁ nipajjitabbaṁ, aggi paricaritabbo, antodevatāpi namassitabbā' ti idaṁ dasavidhaṁ ovādaṁ. (Dhammapada commentary, I., pp. 397-398).

(2) The conversation of slaves and servants is not to be communicated to persons within the household; as such conversation is talked about and causes quarrels.

(3) This means that one should give only to those who return borrowed articles.

(4) This means that one should not give to those who do not return borrowed articles.

(5) This means that one should help poor kinsfolk and friends who look for succour, without considering their capability of repaying.

(6) This means that a wife seeing her mother-in-law or her father-in-law, should stand and not remain sitting.

(7) This means that a wife should not eat before her mother-in-law, father-in-law and husband have taken their meals. She should serve them first, and when she is sure that they have had all they care for, then and not till then may she herself eat.

(8) This means that a wife should not go to bed before her mother-in-law, father-in-law and husband. She should first perform all the duties which she owes them and then she may herself lie down to sleep.

(9) This means that a wife should regard her mother-in-law, father-in-law or husband as a flame of fire or as a serpent-king.

(10) When a monk, after keeping residence in a remote lodging, comes to the door of a house, and the housewife sees him, she must first give to such a

monk whatever food there is in the house, both hard and soft; and then she may eat. (Dhammapada Commy. I., pp. 403-404).

Polygamy and polyandry.

Buddhist literature contains but one reference to polyandry. The only exception indicating the existence of polyandry occurs in the Kuṇāla Jātaka[1] in which we read that princess Kaṇhā was allowed to have at a time five husbands selected by her in a Svayambara assembly. A woman could not marry more than one man at a time nor could a woman as a general rule marry twice in her life, though there were exceptions.[2] We learn from the Nakkhatta Jātaka (no. 49) that on the failure of the selected bridegroom's coming to the bride's house on the appointed day, the bride was given in marriage to another bridegroom. When the first bridegroom came, he was told that the girl could not be married twice over. It was not the custom for a wedded wife to take another mate even if she was not loved by her husband.[3] But there are instances in which married women who were either kidnapped or seduced were kept as wives. While a woman does not generally appear to have taken more than one husband, a man appears to have married more than one woman. In the Vimānavatthu commentary (pp. 149-156) we read that Bhaddā being barren told her husband to marry her sister

---

1. Jātaka, no. 536
2. *Infra*, p. 18.
3. "Ārā dūre na idha kadāci atthi
paramparā nāma kule imasmiṁ.
taṁ kullavattaṁ anuvattamānā
'māhaṁ kule antimagandhinī ahuṁ'
etassa vādassa jigucchamānā
akāmikā baddha carāmi tuyhan ti."
(Kaṇhadīpāyana Jātaka, Fausböll, Jātaka, Vol. IV., p. 35).

Subhaddā. The husband did so. The Babbu Jātaka (no. 137) tells us that a wife delayed in coming back to her husband's house from her father's house and the husband took a second wife. The Ruhaka Jātaka (no. 191) informs us that a husband sent his naughty and deceitful wife away and took a second wife. The Assaka Jātaka (no. 207) gives us another instance of a husband's taking a second wife. In it we read that King Assaka of Potali, a city in the kingdom of Kāsī, took a second queen on the death of his first queen Ubbarī. In some of the Jātakas[1] we find that certain kings had as many as sixteen thousand wives. A Magadhan householder named Magha had four wives at a time, viz, Nandā, Cittā, Sudhammā, and Sujātā (D. C., I., 269). King Bimbisāra had five hundred wives (Mahāvagga, VIII., 1. 15). King Okkāka had five queens (Sumaṅgalavilāsinī, p. 258). The Mahāvaṁsa records that Māyā and Mahāmāyā, two uterine sisters, were given in marriage to Suddhodana (Geiger's Text, p. 14). This is borne out by the fact related in the Tibetan Buddhist books as translated by Rockhill (Life of the Buddha, p. 15) that Suddhodana, in spite of the rigorous provision of the law of the land prohibiting every citizen from marrying more than one woman, was allowed to have two wives as a mark of gratitude for his subduing the hillmen of the Pāṇḍava tribe while a prince. Thus we see that husbands used to take more than one wife in the lifetime of the first wife or after her death. There was no law prohibiting a man taking more than one wife. While the man had the privilege of marrying more than one woman at a time, the woman

1. Jātakas, nos. 514, 538.

had the misfortune of enduring cruel treatment at the hands of her co-wife.

Co-wives.

The worst misery for a woman is to have a co-wife. In almost all cases fellow-wives quarrel with one another and make home a place to fly away from rather than to fly to for peace and comfort. A woman cannot tolerate that her husband should ignore her very existence and take pleasure with other women (Jātaka, no. 519). Sometimes barren women used to bring a second wife for their husbands for the continuance of their husband's line; but the inherent jealousy of women against their co-wives exhibits itself when their co-wives bear children and become husband's favourites. The Dhammapada commentary (I., 45 foll) tells us that the first wife of a householder of Sāvatthī being barren, brought another wife for her husband. When her co-wife became pregnant, she was jealous and effected abortion by administering medicine. Thrice did the woman commit this heinous crime with the result that her co-wife succumbed at last to the effect of the abortive medicine. But the cruel woman did not escape the penalty for doing this sinful deed. She was beaten to death by her husband who declared her to be the cause of the death of his pregnant wife and destroyer of his line. The Petavatthu gives us another illustration. Mattā, the wife of a householder of Sāvatthī was childless. Hence her husband took another wife named Tissā. Being jealous of the rival wife, Mattā, one day, heaped together the sweepings and threw them on the head of her co-wife. Tissā endured humiliation and bad behaviour of her co-wife. On her death Mattā was born as a petī who suffered various miseries. One day she appeared before Tissā and requested her to offer on her account, food, etc., to eight bhikkhus. Tissā bore no grudge against her co-wife despite her ill-behaviour. She did as requested, and Mattā was released from the petaloka. (Paramatthadīpanī on the Petavatthu, pp. 82-89).

Divorce.

Divorce was allowed but without any formal decree. Isidāsī, for instance, had to return twice to her father's house having been turned out of the house by successive husbands because she did not prove agreeable to one husband after another (Therī-Commy. p. 260). No instance is recorded of similar action taken against the husband.

Remarriage of Women.

Certain passages indicate that remarriage of women was not unknown in the Buddhist period. The introduction to the Ucchaṅga Jātaka (no. 67) tells us that a woman's husband, brother and son were once imprisoned. Her loud lamentations caused the king to show her favour. The king said to her, "I give you one of the three, which will you take?" "Sire," was her answer, "If I live, I can get another husband and another son; but as my parents are dead, I can never get another brother. So give me my brother, Sire." This reply of the woman indicates that a woman could probably marry more than once. The instance of Isidāsī, cited above, also illustrates our point.

The Ceylonese Chronicle, Mahāvaṁsa, furnishes us with an instance of widow-remarriage. In it we read that King Khallāṭanāga was overpowered by the commander of his troops named Kammahārattaka. The commander was killed by the King's younger brother named Vaṭṭagāmaṇī. The latter began to rule the kingdom, took his nephew, Mahācūḷika, as his son and made his elder brother's wife, Anulādevī, his queen. (Geiger, Text, pp. 269-270).

Widow-remarriage.

The Avadānakalpalatā of Ksemendra mentions that woman was man's absolute property. Man could dispose of woman in any way he liked. The Avadānakalpalatā tells us that Srīsena, a charitable king of the Ariṣṭā country, had a queen named Jayaprabhā. To fulfil the desire of his preceptor, a disciple came to the king and prayed for queen Jayaprabhā to be given as a preceptor's fee. Srīsena with a smiling face gave away his queen Jayaprabhā. But the preceptor, on receiving the desired fee, changed his mind. He sent back the queen with due respect to the king. (Srīsenāvadāna). In complying with the request of Vāhīkamuni, a disciple of Marīci, Manicūḍa, King of Sāketa, gave away his queen Padmāvatī along with her son to wait upon the old sage (Manicūḍāvadāna). Viśvantara, prince of Viśvapurī, being requested by Indra in a Brahmin's guise, gave away his own wife Mādrī (Viśvantarāvadāna).

Gift of wife.

CHAPTER II

SLAVE GIRLS

Slave girls.

Besides the lawfully married wife and other free-women, there was, in the household, a number of women styled dāsīs or slaves.

Their duties.

Besides her household duties a slave woman had to husk paddy, (D. C., III., 321) pound rice (Jātaka, No. 45) and to go to market. (D. C., I., p. 208).

Marriage.

The Master having full control over his female slaves, his consent was necessary for the latter's marriage. Pasenadi, king of Kosala, had to secure the consent of the master before he could marry Mallikā, daughter of a slave woman of one of the leading Śākya chiefs named Mahānāman.

Manumission.

A slave woman could obtain freedom if she could prove herself worthy of it. The Therīgāthā commentary (pp. 199 ff.) says that Puṇṇā, daughter of Anāthapiṇḍika's domestic slave, was given freedom when she defeated a Brahmin in argument and proved herself to be a woman of religious bent of mind. The Theragāthā indicates that servants were completely at their master's control and mercy. They had no freedom except that given to them by their masters. (Psalms of the Brethren, p. 360; cf. Ibid, p. 22).

Buddha's Influence on slave-girls.

Maid-servants, being of low birth were naturally uncultured and of low spirits. Some of them were in the habit of stealing coins or articles. But the influence of the Buddha's dhamma had a splendid effect on their character. The Dhammapada commentary says that Khujjuttarā, a maid-servant of Sāmāvatī, queen of Udena, king of Kosambī, had to buy flowers daily for eight kahāpaṇas for the queen. But she used to steal four kahāpaṇas daily. One day while she went to the garland-makers' house to buy flowers, she heard the sermon delivered by the Buddha. She obtained sotāpattiphalaṁ. Since then she discontinued stealing and bought flowers for eight kahāpaṇas. The queen questioned her how she had bought so many flowers for eight kahāpaṇas. The maid-servant could no longer conceal anything as by this time her faith in the Buddha had become very strong. She confessed her guilt and said that after hearing the Buddha's sermon she had come to realise that stealing a thing is a sin. The queen asked her to repeat the dhamma she had heard. Khujjuttarā did so in the presence of the queen and her 500 female attendants. The queen did not reproach her for her stealing four kahāpaṇas daily, on the contrary, she praised her much for letting her hear the Buddha's dhamma. Since then the maid-servant was regarded as a mother and teacher by the queen and her 500 female attendants, who asked her to go to the Master daily to hear the dhamma and repeat it to them. In course of time she mastered the Tripiṭaka. (D. C., I., 208 ff).

The Mahāvaṁsa speaks of Bīranī, a maid-servant

engaged by Asoka Brāhmana to give food daily to the Saṁgha which was enough for eight bhikkhus. This she used to do with devotion with the result that after her death she was born in a vimāna in the sky. (Mahāvaṁsa, p. 214).

The maid-servant of a certain lay-disciple who made an arrangement for offering charity to four bhikkhus daily, was ordered to attend on the bhikkhus, prepare seats for them and supply water and other necessary things. The maid-servant served the bhikkhus daily with hearty devotion and observed the precepts of the true dhamma and meditated on the thirty-two impurities for sixteen years as a result of which she was reborn after death as one of the beloved attendants of Sakka. (Vimānavatthu commy, 91-92).

Once the servant-girl of a brahmin living in a brahmin village named Thūṇa in Kosala while going to fetch water saw the Buddha sitting at the foot of a tree. She thought that it was an opportune moment for her to liberate herself from slavery, and being careless whether the brahmins would beat her or even kill her, she offered a pot of water to the Buddha who drank water from it and by his miraculous power the pitcher became full every time its contents were exhausted, so that the disciples quenched their thirst from it. The Buddha in order to increase her faith in him showed that a pot of water given by her was sufficient to quench the thirst of the Buddha and his disciples and he returned the pot full of water to her. The brahmin master heard all about it and was very angry with her and beat her to death. (Vimānavatthu Commentary, pp. 45-47).

The last statement throws a clear light on the position of slave woman and on the treatment they received at the hands of their masters.

Position of female slaves.

The position of female slave was indeed very pitiful. A slave woman, like Roman slave girls, was the property of her master who had every control over her. The treatment of her master or mistress towards her was sometimes most unsatisfactory. She was ill-treated in the majority of cases. The Majjhima Nikāya gives us a painful instance of ill-treatment by the mistress of a house. It says that a woman named Kālī was the maid-servant of a householder's wife named Vedehikā living at Sāvatthī. She was very skilful and capable of doing her duties properly. She was never lazy. Kālī in order to find out whether her mistress's fame was due to her or not once rose late in the morning but her mistress showed her dissatisfaction at this. On the second day she rose up late and was rebuked. On the third day she rose up still very late and she was beaten by her mistress so much that her head was broken. (M. N., I., 125 foll).

The Vimānavatthu commentary furnishes us with another pathetic picture of ill-treatment. A daughter of a brahmin at Gayāgāma became the mistress of her father-in-law's house. She disliked a maid-servant's daughter, whom she hated and used to beat for fault or no fault of hers. Even when the maid's daughter came of age, there was no remission of kicks and blows which became all the more severe as days went on. The fact was that at the time of Kassapa

Buddha the girl had been the mistress and she used to ill-treat and beat her maid who was now born as the Brāhmaṇa lady and the situation was reversed.

The mistress used to punish the maid-servant's daughter by pulling the hair of her head, the maid-servant's daughter, therefore, had the hair of her head shaven by a barber. The mistress tied her head with a rope and punished her and thus the girl came to be called Rajjumālā. At last she went to a forest to commit suicide, unable any more to bear the rude treatment of the mistress. (Vimān. Commy, pp. 206-209).

CHAPTER III

DANCING GIRLS AND COURTEZANS

Dancing girls. The Jātakas refer to dancing girls (nāṭakī) who were accomplished in dancing and music (naccagītavāditakusalā).[1] They were engaged for royal amusement and kept in harem by kings who had as many as sixteen thousand nautch girls (soḷasasu nāṭakisahassesu).[2] The Culla-palobhana Jātaka[3] tells us that a dancing girl was employed by a king to allure his only son who was indifferent to the enjoyment of pleasures, who had no wish for the kingdom and who had never had any dealings whatsoever with women. The dancing girl was young, accomplished in dancing and singing and capable of bringing under her power any man she might come across. She allured the prince by singing "with a voice of honey, so that the music was as sweet as the song, and the song as sweet as the music." The prince listened to her captivating song and desires arose in him gradually. He went the way of the world (lokadhammam sevitvā) and knew the joy of love. So deeply did the prince fall in love with the dancing girl that he would not let another man have this woman. He ran amuck through the streets and attacked the people with a sword. The king had the prince captured and banished him from the city along with the girl. Thus it is seen how the heir-apparent brought up in luxury and ignorant of the ways of women had to undergo

1. Fausböll, Jātaka, II., p. 328; V, p. 249.
2. Ibid., I, p. 437.
3. Ibid., no. 263.

banishment as a penalty for his infatuation for a dancing girl.

Similar allurements were offered to Gautama during his adolescence. Many dancing women were employed to keep the prince in hilarity. They were skilful in dancing and singing and were as lovely as deva-maidens. Clad in beautiful array and ranging themselves in order, these dancing women played upon their musical instruments, danced and sang delightfully. (Rhys Davids, Buddhist Birth Stories, p. 171). References to nautch (dances) occur in the Dīgha Nikāya (Dialogues of the Buddha, I., pp. 5 & 7). Mention is also made of dancing women in the Mahāvaṁsa (p. 227) and the Dhammapada commentary (III., pp. 166 and 297).

Courtesans—their life and character.

The dancing girls usually belonged to that section of the fair sex which had no place by the domestic fireside of the common householder and were reserved for the pleasures of the people. These women earned their livelihood as courtesans. Though they belonged to the tender class, they appear to have lost their inborn feminine qualities by virtue of the abominable way in which they earned their livelihood. They used to attract men by their tempting figure and voice, scents, perfumes and touch, and by their dalliance in strategem. They were like robbers with braided locks, like a poisoned drink, like merchants that sang their own praises, crooked like a deer's horn, evil-tongued like snakes, like a pit that was covered over, like hell which was difficult to fill, like an ogress hard to satisfy, like the all-ravenous

Yama, like all-devouring flame, like all-sweeping river, like wind blowing where it desires, undiscriminating like Mount Meru, and perpetually fruiting like a poison tree.[1] They used to court the man whom they dislified just in the same manner as the man whom they adored. (Cowell., Jātaka, V., p. 242). Being moved by their greed or carnal appetite, they consumed the rich man in whom they were interested, like fuel cast in a blazing fire. (Fausboll, Jātaka, V., p. 452). Frequently they assumed different poses to lure weak-minded people and to cause them to fall a prey to their sinful snare. As soon as they perceived that this was done, they ruined their character, wealth and all by their evil ways. They did not flinch from going so far as to take the lives of persons who used to visit them every night with handsome fees.[2] But the career of certain courtesans mentioned below indicates that vileness in their character did not last long in all cases. Some courtesans appeared to have altered the despicable course of their life through the influence of the Buddha's dhamma and renouncing worldly life they lived an exemplary life with all desires totally uprooted. They strove hard for acquiring merit and finally they could attain Arahatship. Their character as courtesans in the prime of their blooming youth yielded place to saintly character in the later stage of their life and they were held in high esteem by the people.

1. Fausböll, Jātaka, V. p. 425.
2. Cowell, Jātaka, III., p. 40.

Ambapālī.

Ambapālī (Āmrapālī) was born at Vaiśālī in the king's garden at the foot of a mango tree. She was brought up by the gardener of the city. She was known as the Mango-gardener's girl and was named Āmrapālī. When she was grown up, she became perfect in all parts of her body. She was made a courtesan, as there was a law in Vaiśālī that a perfect woman was not allowed to marry, but was reserved for the pleasures of the people. She was beautiful, graceful, pleasant, gifted with the highest beauty of complexion, well versed in dancing, singing and lute-playing and she was much visited by desirous people. She asked fifty (kahāpaṇas) for one night.[1] Bimbisāra, king of Magadha, visited her at Vaiśālī and remained with her for seven days. Āmrapālī was with child by him, and bore him a son who was later on known as Abhaya (fearless). (Cf. Āmrapālyāvadāna in the Avadānakalpalatā). One day Āmrapālī (Ambapālī) heard that the Buddha was at her garden at Vaiśālī. She went to see him. The Buddha preached Dhamma to her and she became pleased with him and invited him to take food in her house. The Licchavis asked Ambapālī to allow the Buddha to take meals at their place but she refused. The Buddha was fed sumptuously by the courtesan. The latter offered her ārāma to the bhikkhusamgha headed by the Buddha who accepted it. Buddha stayed in the ārāma as long as he liked and then went to Veluvagāmaka (Dīgha Nikāya, II., pp. 95-98; cf. Vinaya Piṭaka, I., pp. 231-233). Thereafter when Ambapālī heard her own

---

1 Vinaya Texts, pt. II., p. 171.

son preaching the 'Norm', she tried to acquire insight. The evanescence of her own body was noticed by her and she saw transitoriness in every phenomenon of the universe. At last she attained Arahatship. (Psalms of the Sisters, p. 125).

Padumavatī.

Padumavatī was a courtesan of Ujjain. King Bimbisāra heard of her beauty, came to Ujjain and spent one night with her. Padumavatī told the king that she was with child by him. The king said to her, "If it be a son, let me see him when grown up." He gave her a signet and left her. In due course a son was born. He was named Abhaya. When he was seven years old, he was told that King Bimbisāra was his father. He was sent to the king who loved him and let him grow up with the boys of his court. In course of time he was ordained and attained arahatship. One day his mother heard him preach the Dhamma and renounced the world. In course of time she too attained Arahatship, with thorough grasp of the Dhamma in form and meaning. (Therīgathā Commentary, pp. 39-40).

The incidents in the life of Padumavatī, the courtesan, resemble those in the life of Ambapālī, the courtesan of Vaiśālī. The most funny point of agreement between the two accounts of the lives of two courtesans is that the issues of both these courtesans by one and the same person, viz., Bimbisāra, were known as Abhaya. Of course this does not afford us any strong ground to say that Padumavatī of Ujjenī and Ambapālī of Vaiśālī were one and the same person.

Sālavatī.

There was at Rājagaha, a girl named Sālavatī, who was handsome, graceful, pleasant and exquisitely beautiful. Sālavatī was installed as courtesan by a merchant of Rājagaha. She became expert in dancing singing and lute-playing and was much visited by many people. Her fee was one hundred kahāpaṇas for one night. Before long Sālavatī became pregnant. During her pregnancy she did not allow anybody to visit her on the pretext of illness as pregnant courtesans were not liked by men. In due course a son was born and was thrown into a dust-bin. Early in the morning while going to serve the king, Abhayarājkumāra saw the child surrounded by crows. He was informed by his attendants of the fact that a child was thrown there and was then alive. By the order of the prince, the child was brought to the palace and was nourished by the nurses. The child was named Jīvaka as he was alive when found. He was also named Komārabhacca because he had been caused to be nourished by the royal prince (Komārena posāpito). This Jīvaka Komārabhacca became renowned as the greatest physician of his time. (Vinaya Texts, II. pp., 172-174).

Sirimā.

Sirimā was the daughter of the courtesan, Sālavatī, (Sutta Nipāta commentary, I., 244) and youngest sister of Jīvaka, the well-known physician. She was a courtesan of unique beauty. She lived at Rājagaha. Once she was appointed for a fortnight by the female lay disciple, Uttarā, wife of the treasurer's son Sumana and daughter of the treasurer Puṇṇaka, for one thousand pieces of money per night

(Dhammapada commentary, III., 308-309) in order to minister to Uttarā's husband. One day she offended against Uttarā. Desiring to be on good terms with her again, she begged pardon of her. Uttarā assured her that she would pardon her if the Exalted One would do the same. One day the Master and the congregation of monks came to Uttarā's house. When the Master had finished his meal, Sirimā begged his pardon. The Teacher pronounced thanks-giving and delivered discourses. Sirimā listened to the discourses attentively. Then she attained the first stage of sanctification. Since then she regularly gave alms to eight monks. (Dhammapada commentary, III., 104 foll). The Vimānavatthu commentary says that Sirimā fell ill and died just after her offerings were accepted by a bhikkhu. On her death she was reborn as a celestial nymph and came to worship the Buddha with five hundred female attendants (p. 75). But the Sutta Nipāta commentary (I., p. 244) describes her as reborn in the Yāma heaven as the queen of Suyāma. However, on her death, as we learn from the Dhammapada commentary, Sirimā's dead body was not burnt. It was kept in a charnel-house (āmakasusānaṁ) and watched by a guard against its being devoured by crows and dogs. King Bimbisāra informed the Buddha of her death. The Buddha requested the king not to burn her dead body but to preserve it so that it could be seen by the bhikkhus daily for asubhabhāvanā. The bhikkhus after seeing it daily realised that the most beautiful body becomes rotten, warm eaten and finally the bones remain without flesh. All the citizens were compelled to behold Sirimā's dead body as the royal proclamation was, "All who refuse to do so shall be fined eight pieces of money." This was done with a view to impress on the citizens the idea of transitoriness of human beauty which is but skin-deep. (Dhammapada Commentary, III., 106-109).

Sāmā.

Sāmā was a courtesan of Benares. Her fee was a thousand pieces of money. She was a favourite of the kings and had a suite of five hundred female slaves. She was the cause of the death of a young merchant who was enamoured of her and who used to present her every night with a thousand pieces of money. One day while standing at an open window on the upper floor of her house, she saw a robber, comely, gracious, exceedingly glorious and god-like in appearance, being led along the street. She fell in love with this robber at first sight. She got the robber released by sending a thousand pieces of money to the Governor with the information that the robber was her brother and that he had no other refuge except in Sāma. Thenceforth Sāmā accepted nothing from any other man's hand, but passed all her time, taking her pleasure with this robber only. The robber thought that if this woman should fall in love with any one else she would cause my death also. So he took her with all her ornaments on to a garden, squeezed her till she became insensible and then decamped with all her jewellery, never to return. When Sāmā recovered consciousness she could not find her lord. She fasted for a few days but when she learnt that the robber would not have her, she took once more to her former abominable course of life. (Cowell, Jātaka, III., 40-42).

Sulasā.

In Benares, there lived a beautiful woman of the town named Sulasā. She too like the courtesan Sāmā had a train of five hundred courtesans and her fee was a thousand pieces a night. One day while standing at a window, and looking down on the street she saw a robber named Sattuka being led to the place of execution with his hands bound behind his back. Sulasā loved the robber at first sight and thought, "If I can free that stout-fighting man, I will give up this bad life of mine and live respectably with him." She bribed the chief constable of the city, gained the freedom of the robber and lived with him in delight and harmony, This change in the course of the life of a woman of the town who sells her body for a limited period to different persons is apparently very striking, but really from a psychological standpoint human mind cannot lose its inherent nature by virtue of being placed in loathsome circumstances. The inherent feminine virtue of Sulasā manifested itself when she began to live respectably with a man of her choice. The robber, after three or four months desired to leave her, taking away some of her jewellery. With a view to achieve his end the robber told her that while being hauled along by the king's men he had promised an offering to a tree-deity on a mountain top. Sulasā to fulfil his desire put on all her ornaments and accompanied him to the top of a mountain. She was told there that she had been brought there to be killed and deprived of all her jewellery. She said, "Husband, why would you kill me? I left a rich man's son for you, spent a large sum and saved your life, I might get a thousand pieces a day but I look at no other man. Such a benefactress I am to you; be kind enough to spare my life." The robber heeded not and told her repeatedly that he would kill her. Then Sulasā's wits rose to the occasion. She prayed for the last embrace. Her prayer was granted. She walked round him in respectful salution three times and kissed him. Then she stood behind him as if to do obeisance there and threw him down the precipice, a hundred times as high as a man. The robber was crushed to pieces and died on the spot. Then Sulasā returned home. (Cowell, Jātaka, III., 260-263, cf. Paramatthadīpani on the Petavatthu, p. 4).

Aḍḍhakāsī.

Aḍḍhakāsī was born in the family of a very rich banker of Kāsī. She became a courtesan, but later on she adopted religious life. Once she intended to go to Sāvatthī to receive ordination, but she heard that some wicked people had beset the road, she sent a messenger to the Blessed One who allowed the bhikkhus to confer on her Upasampadā ordination by sending a learned and competent bhikkhuni as messenger. (Vinaya Texts, III., 360-361). She strove hard for insight and in no time she obtained Arahatship with thorough knowledge of the Dhamma in form and meaning. (Therīgāthā commentary, 30-33).

CHAPTER IV

FEMALE CHARACTER

Woman—her character as wife.

Good household wives are always devoted and dutiful to their husbands. They sacrifice their personal comforts and are always ready to undergo all sorts of misery in order to wait upon their beloved husbands. They are called supreme comrades (bhariyā paramā sakhā).[1]

The Sambula Jātaka records an exemplary character of a devoted wife. The husband being attacked with leprosy left the city and came to a forest. The devoted wife, frustrating all attempts of her husband to stop her, followed him to the wilderness to wait upon him. Her devotion to her husband was so very great that being the chief consort of a prince and bred and brought up in luxury, she nursed her diseased husband like one habituated in doing all strenuous household duties. Daily she used to rise early in the morning, sweep out the hermitage, keep some water for her husband to drink, furnish him with a tooth-stick and water to rinse his mouth. She used to ground various medicinal herbs and annoint his sores. Daily she went into the forest with a basket, a spade and a hook to gather wild fruits and herbs. In this way she watched over her husband in the forest till the latter was cured of leprosy. On coming home the ungrateful husband took pleasure with other women and ignored the very existence of this devoted wife who felt this dishonour strongly;

1. Saṁyutta Nikāya, I. p. 37; cf. Kindred Sayings I. p. 52, f.n. 3—"One to whom one may tell a secret that can be told to no one else."

and through jealousy of her rivals she began to grow thin and pale so much so that her veins stood out upon her body. The true devotion which this woman cherished for her husband was given vent to when she said in grief, "A woman may be in splendid attire, but if she be an unloved wife she should put an end to her life by fixing a rope." Such a devotion did not go unrewarded. The devoted wife, at the intervention of an ascetic, regained her former position of honour from her husband. (Jātaka, No. 519).

The Kakkaṭā Jātaka furnishes us with another instance of real devotion to husband. Once some robbers attacked a Sāvatthian landowner and his wife. The robber-chief was deeply moved to see the exquisitely charming and beautiful woman and intended to get her by killing the husband. The woman was a good, virtuous and devoted wife. She fell at the robber's feet crying, "My lord, if you kill my husband for love of me, I will take poison, or stop my breath and kill myself too. I will not go with you. Do not kill my husband." Thus the woman succeeded in saving herself and her husband. (Jātaka, no. 267).

Instances of virtuous women may easily be multiplied. Thus we hear of Sujātā, a faithful, virtuous and dutiful girl who properly discharged her duty to her husband and parents-in-law (Jātaka, no. 194). Asitābhu was another good and beautiful wife. She was not taken care of by her husband who used to enjoy himself elsewhere. She took no notice of this indifference. She invited the two chief disciples of the Buddha, made them presents and listened to their teachings, until she obtained the fruit of the First Path. At last thinking that her husband had no need of her, she embraced religious life and in course of time became a saint (Jātaka, no. 234). Rāhula's mother was another devoted wife. She renounced worldly life on her husband's and son's embracing religious life (Jātaka, no. 281). A truly devoted wife pines away for the loss of her dear husband. Kosaladevī, for instance, died of love for her husband who was deprived of his life by his own son. (Jātaka, no. 239). Good wives do not like that their husbands should leave them and embrace ascetic life. Some women whose husbands had joined the order, dressed themselves in their finery and with child in arms tried in various ways to seduce their ascetic husbands from the order, but they were unsuccessful. (Psalms of the Brethren, pp. 15-16, 184 & 226). One of them listening to her husband's words, was deeply moved and thought of the uselessness of leading a domestic life being deserted by her husband. She then renounced worldly life and joined the order of sisters. (Ibid., p. 14).

A husband is a woman's 'emblem and sign' (bhattā paññānaṁ itthiyāti (Saṁyutta Nikāya, pt. 1., p. 42). "Even though she be an emperor's daughter, once married a woman is known as so—and so's wife. There are, however, several cases where she is called so and so's mother, or famed under her own name though married, e.g., Visākhā (Kindred Sayings, I. p. 58, f. n. 3). Woman is the 'Commodity supreme' (itthi bhaṇḍānaṁ uttamaṁ).[1]

The Buddha himself says, "A daughter may be

1. Saṁyutta Nikāya, I., p. 43. "Because she is of indispensable utility or because through her Bodhisats and world-rulers take birth."—Commentary. (Kindred sayings, pt. 1., p. 62. f. n. 1).

better than a son if she is intelligent, virtuous, devoted to her husband and parents-in-law. She may even rule a kingdom.[1] The issue of such a good daughter may become a hero and ruler of some countries. (Samyutta Nikāya, pt. 1., p. 86).

Female wickedness.

As there are good household wives so are there bad and wicked wives as well. There are twenty-five different ways in which a wicked woman is to be known. She praises her lord's absence from home, she is not pleased at his return, she speaks ill of him, she is silent in his praise, she acts to his injury and not to his profit, she does what ought not to be done but she never does what ought to be done, she goes to bed with her clothes on and lies with her face turned away from him, she changes her side frequently, she makes a great ado, she sighs a long drawn sigh, she feels a pain, she has to solicit nature at frequent intervals, she acts perversely, she lends her ear to a stranger's voice and listens attentively. She wastes her husband's goods, she forms an intimacy with her neighbours, she wanders abroad, she walks along the streets, she is guilty of adultery, she treats her husband with disrespect, she exposes herself shamelessly to passers-by and standing at the door she often looks around with a confused mind. (Fausböll, Kunāla Jātaka, V., pp. 434-435).

There are nine grounds on which a woman incurs blame. If she is fond of frequenting pleasure parks, gardens, river banks and houses of relatives or of

1. References to women rulers are found in the Mahāvaṁsa. Queen Anulā herself reigned for four months. (Ch. 34, śl. 27). Sīvalī, daughter of Āmaṇḍa and younger sister of Cūlābhaya reigned for four months (Ch. 35, śl. 14).

strangers, if she dresses herself in smart cloth vest, if she is addicted to strong drink, if she stares about her with idle looks or stands before her door. A wicked woman despises her lord on eight grounds: If the husband be poor or sick or old or a habitual drunkard, or reckless or dull, or overworked by his cares of business or disobliging. (Fausböll, Jātaka, V., 433).

Wicked wives are not satisfied with their lot. They are very exacting. Somehow or other they will have the thing which they are in need of. Husband's poverty is no consideration to them. Once a poor man's wife intended to go to a festival putting on a safflower-coloured cloth but the husband was too poor to get it. The wife was so obstinate that she did not hear her husband's pleadings for poverty but she caused her husband to risk his life in stealing safflower from the conservatories. (Jātaka, no. 147). A wicked wife feigns sickness and does not do her household duties. In vain her husband tries to get her cured of her ailment. (Jātaka, no. 130).

The Kaccāni Jātaka (no. 417) furnishes us with a picture of how strife and discontent prevail in a house owing to the young wife's trick. Young wives do not like to wait upon old mothers-in-law but they try to poison their husbands' ears against their mothers-in-law. (cf. Jātaka, no. 446).

The Culla-Paduma Jātaka tells us that a wife was tired of walking and was carried on shoulder by her husband. In course of journey she became so very thirsty that the husband at last struck his right knee and the wife quenched her thirst by drinking blood from the right knee of her husband. They then came to the bank of the Ganges and began to live in a hut. One day the husband saw a robber with hands, feet, nose and ears cut off, drifting down the stream with loud wailing. The husband took pity on him, brought him ashore and cured him. Now the wife fell in love with this stranger and devised a plan to kill her husband. She took her husband to the top of a mountain and in the pretext of offering something to the spirit of the hill, she smote him on the back and hurled him down the precipice. Then she returned home with great joy. (Jātaka, no. 193). This is an appalling instance of an ungrateful and treacherous wife. The husband quenched the thirst of his wife with the blood of his own person but he could not win her sinful heart. On the contrary he had to pay the price of his goodness in the shape of loss of his life at the hand of his own wife. Such awful instances of wife's ingratitude and lechery are numerous in the Jātakas. The Vinaya Texts furnish us with an instance of a wife's infidelity. A certain woman, while her husband was away from home, became pregnant as a result of her intrigues with a paramour. She had a premature delivery and got the fœtus carried away by a bhikkhuṇī, a confederate of hers. pt. III., 345).

The Saundarananda Kāvya of Aśvaghoṣa fairly depicts the character of women. It points out that women subdue gods, kings and sages by their amorous gestures, pride, movement, grace, smile, wrath, infatuation and speech. (Saundarananda Kāvya, Canto. VII., Śl, 24). Infatuated women cause passionate excitement in men and when infatuation is over, they cause fear. They are never worthy to be attended to. They cause dissension amongst relatives and friends. They are fond of speaking ill of others. They are wrong-doers. They earn commendation by their speech and cause pain with their sharp mind. Their words are as sweet as honey but their heart is full of subtle venom. It is difficult to win minds of women. As a poisonous creeper, an unsheathed sword, and shelter in a cave inhabited by reptiles are causes of danger and death, so do women cause future danger. Women are the cause of good men's taking to impoverished life, of their doing hazardous deeds and of their running rapidly in front of soldiers for battle. Physical beauty, wealth, intelligence, lineage or prowess are of no consideration to women who bring about ruin without any consideration like rivers full of acquatic animals. Women do not remember sweet words, caressing and friendship. There is no one more crooked than fickle women. Women give pleasure to those who do not give them anything in return, they are violent to those who give them much, they are proud to those who bow down their head to them but they are pleased with haughty persons. They forget past friendship and take pleasure with new men just as cows wounded in one field graze happily in another. If husbands be qualified then wives treat them as husbands, if they possess no merit, then wives behave like enemies. If they be rich then wives follow them through greed, but if they be poor then wives treat them with contempt. Though women embrace self-immolation on their husband's funeral pyre or voluntarily sacrifice their life, yet they do not suffer for their husbands, because heartily they do not love anybody. A few women serve their husbands as gods; but thousands of women satisfy their own heart through fickle-mindedness. (Saundarananda Kāvya, Canto VIII).

The Buddhist literature depicts the bright as well as the dark side of female character. It gives us a vivid picture of the inherent nature of the tender sex. The brightness of feminine virtue is reflected specially in the lives of bhikkhunis and theris. It is indeed remarkable that tenderness of women could endure the hardship of religious life. The dark side of female character as portrayed in the Buddhist literature, excites terror and hatred though the delineation is a correct representation of facts. People, having got all the terrible traits in the character of the tender sex in one place, cannot entertain respectful feelings towards women. They are apt to cherish frightful feelings and to keep themselves aloof from feminine charms that overcome man's reason. The softness of feminine heart could awfully assume stone-like hardness by sacrificing motherly feelings in attempting to murder a child (D. C. I., pp. 174 foll). The Mahāvaṁsa furnishes us with another instance of woman's criminal nature. It tells us that the queen of Devānampiyatissa coveted the kingship for her own son and went so far as to take the life of her husband's younger brother, the vice-regent named Mahānāga by offering a poisonous mango which, unfortunately for the lady and fortunately for Mahānāga, was eaten by the little son of the queen with a fatal result. (ch. 22) The ways of women cannot be understood easily. They are as perplexing as the course of a fish in the sea. (Jātaka, no. 519). Frail as women are, they are of fickle mind which is as changing as that of shifty monkeys, as the shade cast by a tree on height or depth around, and as the tire of wheel revolving swift without a pause or rest. Women are insensible to parents' love and ties of brotherhood. They do not hesitate in playing a shameless part and are ever ready to violate every law of right. They follow the dictates of their own mind in all their deeds. (Fausböll, Jātaka, V., p. 445). Their only weapons are speech, smiles, dance and song. They harass unstable minds (Fausböll, Jātaka, V., 452). They are as deadly as black serpents' head and as ravenous as fire. (Fausböll, Jātaka, V., p. 446). They are full of seductive strategem and deceitful. They never tell the truth for truth amongst them is very rare (saccaṁ sudullabhaṁ). They hold truth for falsehood and falsehood for truth. (musā tāsam yathā saccaṁ saccaṁ tāsam yathā musā, Fausböll, Jātaka, I., p. 295, cf. Ibid. V., p. 94). In speech, they make no distinction between the false and true. (Cowell, Jātaka, V., p. 242). Like fuel burning in a blazing fire they burn the man whom they serve for gold or for desire. (Fausböll, Jātaka, II., p. 330; cf. Jātaka, no. 536). They are pleasure-seekers and unrestrained in lust. (Fausböll, Jātaka, V., 435 and 448). They are so passionate that no guard can keep them right. They cannot be restrained from going after their desires. The preamble to the Mudupāṇi Jātaka (Fausböll, vol. II, p. 323) says that wise men of old could not guard their own daughters. While daughters stood holding their father's hands, they escaped with their paramours without their fathers' knowledge (porāṇakapaṇḍitāpi attano dhītaraṁ rakkhituṁ nāsakkhiṁsu, pitaraṁ hatthe gahetvā ṭhitā va pitaraṁ ajānāpetvā kilesavasena purisena saddhiṁ palāyīti). Women cannot be guarded. A woman was kept in mid-ocean in a palace in the Simbali lake but she could not preserve her honour. She went wrong in spite of the strong guard (porāṇakapaṇḍitā mātugāmaṁ mahāsamuddamajjhe simbalidahavimāne vasāpetvāpi rakkhituṁ nāsakkhiṁsu. Fausböll, Jātaka, III. p. 90; cf. Ibid., p. 187). A girl was brought up entirely by women from her birth. She saw no man other than her husband. She was kept in a seven-storied house which had seven gateways at each of which was kept a strong guard of women only. But such a girl sinned with an outsider who was brought in with the girl's consent by her designing waiting woman. The girl corrupted herself and took to various tricks to prove her innocence (Fausböll, Jātaka, I., 289-295). The Gahapati Jātaka (no. 199) gives us another instance of a wife's playing tricks with her husband in whose absence she used to intrigue with the village headman. The Ucchiṭṭha-Bhatta-Jātaka (no. 212) tells us that a wicked wife used to intrigue with another man in her husband's absence. She was so very treacherous that she gave cold rice to her husband while she entertained her paramour with hot rice. Her crime was soon discovered and she was severely punished for her heinous offence. The Durājāna Jātaka (no. 64) says that a sinful and wicked woman who used to misconduct herself would become as meek as a slave on the days she would go wrong but on the days she did no wrong, she was found to be a passionate and tyrannical mistress. (cf. Jātakas, nos. 145, 198 and 262). A bride while carried in a closed carriage accompanied by a large escort misconducted herself with King

Kaṇḍari of Benares who was kept concealed by his minister in a tent-shaped screen in order to be convinced of the depravity of womankind (Fausböll, Jātaka, V., p. 439). Passion to women is all-consuming. Women are proud by nature. They will not let their pride kiss the ground easily by a man whom their heart yearns for. Once a handsome woman seeing a handsome land-owner fell in love with him at first sight. The passion within her was like a fire burning her body through and through. She lost her senses, both of body and mind; she cared nothing for food; she only lay down hugging the frame of the bedstead. Her friends and handmaidens with great difficulty secured the man's consent to enjoy company with the woman. The woman prepared her chamber, and dressed herself in her finery and sat on the bed waiting until the man came and sat down beside her. Then a thought came to her mind: "If I accept his address at once, and make myself cheap, my pride will be humbled. To let him have his will the very first day he comes, would be out of place. I will be capricious to-day and afterwards I will give way." So no sooner had he touched her, and begun to dally, she caught his hands and spoke roughly to him, bidding him go away, as she did not want him. He shrank back angrily and went off home. Thereafter repeated requests failed to bring the man back and the woman at last pined away and died. (Fausböll, Jātaka, II., 337-340). The Bandhanamokkha Jātaka (no. 120) tells us that a queen had, by her unceasing importunity, caused a king to promise that he should not look on any other woman with eyes of love, but she herself used to sin in the absence of the king. She sinned with sixty-four messengers who were sent to her by the king on his way to and from the frontier to enquire how she was doing and also to inform her how he (the king) was keeping. On the king's return the queen's crime was soon discovered. The chaplain of the king asked his majesty not to punish the queen as the passions of women are insatiate and she (the queen) had acted according to her innate nature. Kinnarā, chief queen of Benares, misconducted herself with a 'loathsome mishappen cripple' (Fausböll, Jātaka, V. pp. 437-438). Their position as queens could not restrain their lewdness. Woman is profligacy incarnate (itthiyo asātā nāma).[1] Fired and blinded by their unbridled lust women do not shrink from misconducting themselves with their own son nor do they step backward to take away the life of their own sons whom they suckled at their own breast in order to sin freely with men of their choice. The Asātamanta Jātaka[2] says that a blind and decrepit woman hearing of her own praise from a pupil of her son thought that the pupil had fallen in love with her. Passion was kindled within her (andhāya jarājiṇṇāya abbhantare kileso uppajji). So one day removing the curtain of shame she said to the pupil, "Do you desire to play amorous sport with me?" (mayā saddhiṁ abhiramituṁ icchasīti). The pupil answered in the affirmative and said that his strict master was on the way. The woman said, "If you desire me, I shall kill my son" (puttaṁ me mārehīti). Thus settled the old woman, one night with the help of a string as her guide, proceeded with an axe to take away the life of her dutiful son. She actually lay down her axe on the throat of a wooden figure feeling it to her son's. "So

1. Fausböll, Jātaka, Vol. I., p. 288.
2. Ibid., pp. 285-288.

lustful, vile and degraded are women, that, giving the rein to lust, a hag like this, and old as she was, actually thirsted for the blood of so dutiful a son!" (Cowell, Jātaka, I., p. 149).

The Avadānakalpalatā furnishes us with appalling instances of woman's lewdness. Kāmakalā, wife of Candandatta, a merchant of Ujjain, became very lustful on her husband's going abroad for trade. She intended to go out of the house to satisfy her passion, but she was advised by her maid-servant to remain in the house and to satisfy her desires secretly. The diplomacy of her maid-servant brought about union with her own son, Aśvadaṇḍa, in a dark place. After a few days union, she made herself known to her son who by her advice murdered his father on his return and went to a foreign country with his mother. There Aśvadaṇḍa and Kāmakalā lived as husband and wife. But the infidelity of Kāmakalā towards her husband did not stop here. Kāmakalā was charmed with the beauty of a merchant's son named Sundar and had clandestine union with him But she was detected by her son and she had to pay the price of her second infidelity in the shape of loss of her life at the hands of her own son. (Dharmaruci Avadāna.)

Tiṣyarakṣā, wife of the Emperor Aśoka, was moved by the beauty of her step-son Kuṇāla. Removing the curtain of shame, she begged love of Kuṇāla but was rebuked and turned off. Enraged at this she entertained evil thoughts against him. At this time Kuṇāla was sent by the Emperor to conquer Taksaśīlā. There he stayed for sometime. Meanwhile the Emperor Aśoka fell ill and on the physician's failure to cure the emperor, Tiṣyarakṣā herself treated the emperor and cured him. Then the emperor wished to grant a boon to his empress. Tiṣyarakṣā prayed for the kingdom for seven days. The prayer was granted. Having the royal prerogative Tiṣyarakṣā sent a royal letter to Kuñjarkarna of Takṣaśīlā asking him to uproot the eyes of Kuṇāla and drive him out of the kingdom in a nude state. Kuṇāla saw the letter and uprooted his own eyes. Then with his wife Kāñcanmālā, Kuṇāla left Takṣaśīlā and took to beggar's life. After a long time he came to Pāṭaliputra and took shelter in the royal elephant shade. Aśoka heard the sound of his song and lute and recognised him as his own son. He learnt everything about Tiṣyarakṣā from Kuṇāla and became angry. He was about to inflict proper punishment but he forgave her at Kuṇāla's request. (Kuṇāla Avadāna).

Śikhaṇḍi, king of Rouruka country was overwhelmed with grief for having murdered his father. To dispel his sorrow, his mother said, "Śikhaṇḍi was stealthily begotten by another man. So he is not guilty of parricide." (Udrāyanāvadāna). The queen-mother's statement to alleviate the grief of the king casts a slur on her character and furnishes us with a picture of the royal harem being sometimes secretly dishonoured by wicked persons. Once a minister in attendance on the king of Benares misconducted himself in the royal harem. He was banished by the king who witnessed this heinous offence with his own eyes. (Jātaka, no. 303). Pañcapāpā, well-known for her being soft to the touch, became queen of two kings, who enjoyed her company for seven days by turn. She dwelt seven days in the house of one of them, and then crossed over in a ship to the abode of the other, and when in mid-stream she misconducted herself with the pilot, a lame and bald old man, who steered the vessel. (Fausböll, Jātaka, V., p. 440 foll).

The misconduct of queen Pīṅgiyāni with a royal groom is another instance of a woman's infidelity. When the king fell asleep every night she used to get down through the window, misconduct herself with the groom and then she used to climb back to the palace and shampooned her person with perfumes and lay down with the king. The coolness of her person at midnight caused suspicion in the king's mind. The king one day watched her conduct, detected her faithlessness and punished her properly. Being the wife of Brahmadatta, 'earth's all conquering lord', Piṅgiyāni sinned with her devoted husband's slave and lost by lewdness both king and knave. (Fausböll, Jātaka, V., 444).

The queen of King Tissa of Kalyāṇī, was in intrigue with her husband's younger brother named Ayya-uttika. The liaison was discovered by the king. Ayya-uttika fled from the kingdom but nothing is mentioned about any punishment inflicted on the queen by the king. (Mahāvaṁsa, p.171). A queen was in intrigue with her husband's younger brother known as Abhayanāga who in course of time slew the king and himself became king with his elder brother's wife as his queen. (Ibid., p. 309). Anulā, an infamous queen, fell in love successively with a palace guard, a city carpenter, a wood-carrier and the royal priest and misconducted herself with each of them and caused, by turn, the death of each of their lives by poison. (Ibid., pp.279 ff). The example of this licentious Anulā is an illustration of woman's carnal appetite that knows no satisfaction and that makes her a murderess.

All women fail to find delight in their own abode. A wife forsakes her husband though he might be strong and lusty. She will sin with any other man even with a lame person. (Fausböll, Jātaka, V., p.440). She cannot be trusted even if she has borne ten children (na vissase itthi dasanna mātaraṁ, Fausböll, Jātaka, V., 448). A woman having eight husbands, strong and submissive to her will and capable of fulfilling love's duties, will yet set her love on the ninth for she still wants something. (Fausböll, Jātaka, V. 450). Women desire rich lovers like cows greedily seeking new pastures. (gāvo bahutiṇasseva omasanti varaṁ varaṁ, (Ibid., p. 446; cf. Fausböll, Jātaka, I., 295). They can hardly stick to one man (Jātaka, no. 507). If they get secrecy and opportunity at the same time, every single of them would fall from virtuous paths. On the failure of other lovers, they will not pause to sin with a humpback dwarf.[1] They even go so far as to cause defilement in sanctified souls and overcome the virtue of ascetics by their feminine charms and passionate pose (Jātakas, nos. 63, 263, 507, 523 & 526). They look as fair as lotus flowers. Their budding charms stir up sensuous desire in the minds of laymen as well as ascetics, and make them mad (Jātakas, nos. 66, 523 and 527). They tempt one with looks and smiles, another by their walk; some

1. Sace labbhetha khaṇaṁ vā raho vā nivātakaṁ vāpi labbhetha tādisaṁ sabbā ca itthī karreyyuṁ no pāpaṁ aññaṁ aladdhā piṭhasappināpi (saddhiṁ) Fausböll, Jātaka, V. p. 435).

by strange disguise and others by honeyed words. (Jātaka, no, 536).

There are forty different ways a woman makes up to a man. She displays activity, she bends down, she leaps playfully, she looks bashful, she presses together her finger tips, she places one foot on the other, she scratches the ground with a stick, she dances her boy up and down, she plays and makes the boy play, she kisses and makes the boy kiss her, she eats and gives him to eat, she gives or begs something, whatever is done she imitates, she speaks in a high or low voice. she speaks indistinctly at one time and distinctly at another time, she appeals to him with dance, song and music, with tears or attempts to attract admiration, or with her fineries she laughs or stares, she shakes her dress, she moves her loin-cloth, exposes or covers up her leg, exposes her bosom, her armpit, her navel, she closes her eyes, she raises her eyebrow, she pinches her lips, her tongue, she makes her tongue loll out, she looses or tightens her cloth, looses or tightens her head dress. (Fausböll, Jātaka, V., pp. 433-434). Five kinds of women, such as a clever woman, a beautiful woman, a neighbour's wife, a woman who is admired by many men and a woman who seeks a man of weatlh for mate, should be shunned by every man. (Ibid., p. 446). Women in highways, in lordly halls, in royal cities or in small townships should be avoided. A man who may be famous, wise or respected by all people, will lose his glory like the Moon eclipsed by Rāhu if he happen to come under a woman's sway. (Ibid. p. 453).

We have just given a terrible picture of woman's inborn nature as drawn in the Buddhist literature. We have found how women disregarding their social status and the pecuniary circumstances in which they were put in, used to commit sin and trick their husbands. Sinful women when detected had to undergo punishment for their clandestine corruption which deserved death, imprisonment, mutilation or cleaving asunder. (Vadhabandhanachejjabhejjāraham dosam, Fausböll, Jātaka, V., p. 444). But they were, in no case, divorced on the ground of adultery, though divorce was not unknown in those days. The severe punishments that were inflicted on women for the violation of chastity, go to show that chastity was held in high esteem in those days.

The lechery and the infidelity of womankind as delineated above, do not warrant the inference that female chastity was not seriously observed. On the contrary, female chastity finds a very important place in the Buddhist literature. The Mahāparinibbāṇa Suttanta of the Dīgha Nikāya tells us in connection with the Licchavis that violation of chastity was a serious offence. The punishment for a woman who broke her marriage vow was so very severe that the husband could with impunity take away her life. Speaking of the Licchavis, Buddha himself says that "no women or girls belonging to their clan are detained among them by force or abduction." In the Aṇḍabhūta Jātaka we meet with a reference to the ordeal of fire to prove chastity. (Saccakiriyaṁ katvā aggiṁ pavisitvā tumhe saddahāpessāmīti, Fausböll, Jātaka, I., 294). From the

Mahāummagga Jātaka (no. 546) we learn that a bride-groom married a bride after testing her chastity in the following way:—

He sent some of his men with a thousand pieces of money and told them to test the woman whom he had caused to sit down in the gatekeeper's house, telling the gatekeeper's wife of his plan. The men did so as they were bid. But the women when offered the money refused to accept it saying, "This is not worth the dust of my master's feet." The men came back and said everything to the bride-groom. Thrice the men were sent but thrice did they return with the same answer. The fourth time he asked his men to drag her away by force. They did so, but when the bride saw the bride-groom in a new dress she could not recognise him but smiled and wept at the same time as she looked at him. When questioned, she replied that she had smiled when she had beheld magnificence thinking that this magnificence must have been earned for some good deed in a former life, and that she had wept in pity thinking that such a magnificent man would go to hell for sinning against the property watched and tended by another. After this reply she was proved to be a woman chaste in body and mind.

The Madulakkhaṇa Jātaka (no. 66) furnishes us with a plausible account of ready wit and intelligence displayed by a woman in preserving her chastity. Once an ascetic saw a queen in beautiful dress. He broke through the higher morality and gazed upon her. Lust was kindled within him. Since then he lay on his wooden couch in his hut for seven days as a prey to hunger and thirst, being enslaved by the queen's grace. On the seventh day the king went to the hut and found the ascetic lying on his couch. Questioned by the king as to his ailment, the ascetic told the king openly that he was fired by lust for the queen. The king offered his queen to the sage to fulfill his lustful desire, but as he was giving her away, the king secretly told the queen to put forth her utmost endeavour to save the holy man. When the queen came out of the palace, she asked the sage to go to the king and arrange for a house for them to live in. The sage did so; then the queen entered the house and ordered the sage many times to do many things one after another. But the ascetic did not get tired. As he sat with her upon the bed she took him by the whiskers and drew him towards her till they were face to face. Then she said, "Have you forgotten that you are a holy man and a brāhmin?" This querry brought the ascetic to his senses, and saved the queens chastity. The ascetic forsook all lustful desire and took the queen to the king. (cf. Account of Jayaprabhā in Srīsenāvadāna in Avadānakalpalatā).

A chaste woman who followed her diseased husband in a forest to wait upon him, was once seized by a goblin in the forest while returning to her hut with wild fruits. The woman was told by the goblin to obey him or to lose her life. But she said that it was not a matter of grief for her that she should fall a prey to an abominable ogre, but that the love for her dear husband should fall away from her. (Fausböll, Jātaka, V., p. 88 et. seq., cf. Kakkaṭā Jātaka, no. 267). This is indeed a pious expression of a woman pure in mind and body and truly devoted to her beloved husband.

Strīratna.

The ideal woman is described by the Buddha himself in the Mahā-Sudassana Suttanta of the Dīgha Nikāya. There the Buddha says that the woman who is handsome, beautiful in appearance, pleasing in manner and of the most fine complexion; neither too tall, nor too short, neither too thin, nor too fat, neither too dark, nor too fair, and who possesses divine beauty surpassing human beauty, is an itthiratana, a jewel among women. (Dīgha Nikāya, vol. II. p. 175). Exactly similar idea about a jewel among women is expressed in a Sanskrit Mahāyāna work, named Lalitavistara. Here we read that one who resembles a woman, who belongs to the Kṣatriya caste, who is neither too long nor too short, neither too fat nor too thin, neither too fair nor too dark, pleasing, amiable, handsome, the pores of whose skin emit sandal smell, and whose mouth gives out lotus smell, is called a strīratna or a jewel among women. (Lalitavistara, p. 17).

Different types of wife.

The Buddhist literature speaks of different types of wife. The following presents a set of seven kinds of wife :—

(1) Wife who is a murderess.
(2) Wife who is a thief.
(3) Wife who lords over her husband.
(4) Wife who is kind to her husband like a mother.
(5) Wife who likes her husband as a sister likes her brother.

(6) Wife who is like a female friend.
(7) Wife who is like a maid-servant.

There is another set of seven types which may be mentioned as follows:—

(1) Wife who is always angry, hot-tempered, wishing ill of her husband, who is attached to others, who does not care for her husband, who is always ready to kill her husband if opportunity arises.
(2) Wife who steals the earnings of her husband.
(3) Wife who is lazy, does not mind to work, rough, hot-tempered, who uses harsh words, who wants to lord over the remaining members of the family including her husband.
(4) Wife who is kind to her husband as a mother to her son, always protects her husband and also protects the earnings of her husband.
(5) Wife who behaves with her husband like an elder sister with her younger sister, who is always bashful, who is devoted to her husband.
(6) Wife who finds delight in seeing her husband like a female companion seeing her friend after a long time, who upholds the tradition of the family.
(7) Wife who is not angry in any sphere of life even if beaten and oppressed by her husband, who always pardons her husband with a loving heart and who is always devoted to her husband as a maid-servant to her master. (Aṅguttara Nikāya, IV. pp. 92-93).

Seven kinds of wife.

In the Sujāta Jātaka (no. 269). Buddha himself classifies wives into seven kinds* which are as follows :—

(1) A wife who is bad-hearted, relentless to the good, hates her husband but loves others and who is a destroyer of everything that is obtained at the expense of her husband's wealth. Such a wife is called Destructive wife.

(2) A wife who steals something from whatever her husband obtains for her by trade or skilled profession or the farmer's spade. Such a woman is designated as Thievish wife.

---

* Paduṭṭhacittā ahitānukampinī
aññesu rattā atimaññāte patiṁ
dhanena kītassa vadhāya ussukā,
yā evarūpā purisassa bhariyā
"vadhakā ca bhariyā" ti ca sā pavuccati.
Yaṁ itthiyā vindati sāmiko dhanaṁ
sippaṁ vaṇijjañ ca kasiṁ adhiṭṭhaham
appam pi tasmā apahātum icchati,
yā evarūpā purisassa bhariyā
"corī ca bhariyā" ti ca sā pavuccati.
Akammakāmā alasā mahagghasā
pharusā ca caṇḍī duruttavādinī
upaṭṭhāyikānaṁ abhibhuyya vattati,
yā evarūpā purisassa bhariyā
"ayyā ca bhariyā" ti ca sā pavuccati.
Yā sabbadā hoti hitānukampinī
mātā va puttaṁ anurakkhate patiṁ
tato dhanaṁ sambhatam assa rakkhati,
yā eva rūpā purisassa bhariyā
"mātā ca bhariyā" ti ca sā pavuccati.
Yathāpi jeṭṭhā bhaginī kaniṭṭhakā
sagāravā hoti sakamhi sāmike
hirīmanā bhattuvasānuvattinī
yā evarūpā purisassa bhariyā
"bhaginī ca bhariyā" ti ca sā pavuccati.
Yā c' īdha disvāna patiṁ pamoditā
sakhī sakhāram va cirassa āgataṁ
kolīniyā sīlavatī patibbatā,
yā evarūpā purisassa bhariyā
"sakhī ca bhariyā" ti ca sā pavuccati.
Akkuṭṭhasantā vadhadaṇḍatajjitā
aduṭṭhacittā patino titikkhati
akkodhanā bhattuvasānuvattinī,
yā evarūpā purisassa bhariyā
"dāsī ca bhariyā" ti ca sā pavuccati.

(Fausböll, Jātaka, vol. II., pp. 347-348).

(3) A wife who is lazy, passionate, covetous, foulmouthed, full of anger and abhorrence, careless of duty and oppressive to her subordinates. Such a woman is termed High and Mighty wife.

(4) A wife who sympathises with the good, takes a motherly care of her husband and guards everything her husband brings. Such a wife obtains the designation of "Motherly wife".

(5) A wife who is modest, obedient to her husband's will and respects her husband like a young sister paying homage to elders. Such a wife is called Sisterly wife.

(6) A wife who is virtuous, comes of a high family, takes such a pleasure in husband's sight as a friend takes in seeing a friend after long absence and depends entirely upon her husband. Such a woman is called a Friendly wife.

(7) A wife who is patient, passionate, true to her heart, quiet when abused, afraid of violence and submissive to her husband's will. Such a wife acquires the title of Slavish wife.

A wife should perform her duties by hospitality to the kin of both by faithfulness, by watching over the goods he brings, and by skill and industry in discharging all her business. (Dialogues, III., 182). The Aṅguttara Nikāya speaks of certain qualities which every woman should be endowed with. For example, she must be obedient to her husband, must use sweet words to him, must act according to his liking, she should honour and worship her husband's gurus, e. g., her mother-in-law, father-in-law, samaṇas, and brāhmaṇas, she should

Qualities of a dutiful house-wife.

welcome guests and look after their comfort, she should be skilled in spinning and weaving and she must not be lazy in doing household duties. She must adopt means to finish the household duties; must be intelligent enough to do and manage household affairs, must look after the work of the menial servants and employees in the house; must make arrangement for their treatment during illness and for food; must preserve the earnings of the husband, must not steal husband's earnings, must not deceive the husband, must not waste money by drinking wine or by other bad means, must take refuge in the three gems, must be observers of five precepts, must be charitable, must be liberal and not stingy. (A. N., IV., pp. 268-269). The Dhammapada commentary (III., p. 41) tells us that fetching water, pounding rice and cooking were some of the duties of a household woman.

Mention is made of four qualities which enable a woman to obtain victory in the next world. (Paralokavijayāya paṭipanno hoti). (A. N., IV., p. 270).

1. Skill in household duties: a woman must not be lazy. She must be able, to spin yarn and weave cloth from wool and cotton. She must know the time of performing different household duties.

2. Capacity to look after members of the family: She must take care of her husband's servants, maid-servants and other employees. She must see that they perform their duties properly. She must look after them when they are ill. She must supply proper food to them.

3. Capability of doing everything to the liking of her husband. She must not do that even, at the sacrifice of her life, which is not liked by her husband.

4. Thrift: She should save the earnings of her husband; She must save wealth, gold, silver, corn, etc., earned by her husband. She must not steal them, must not spend them for drinking, gambling and other purposes.

A woman possessed of these virtues, devoted to the Buddha, Dhamma and Samgha, observer of precepts, charitable and wise, must be happy in the next world. (A. N., IV., pp. 269-271).

CHAPTER V

FEMALE EDUCATION

From the account of women who came under the influence of Buddhism it would appear that they could follow religious teachings and were not altogether steeped in ignorance. As a matter of fact some women of the Buddhist period were not behind their male brothers in education. Buddhist literature does not contain any reference to unmarried girls being sent to school or being schooled at home. But there are references to many educated women. The verses in the Therīgāthā are attributed, in the tradition of the Pāli canon, to certain saintly sisters; and we are not entitled to entertain any doubt about Indian women's erudition. The religious harangue of Sukkā and the philosophical discussion of Khemā and Dhammadinnā may be cited here as instances of Indian women's attainments; to ignore the reality of which is to wilfully disregard the quantum of historical truth buried deep in the Buddhist literature. Names of certain ancient Indian women notable for their scholarship are still in the living memory of the present generation, Indian if not European. But then it is still disputed on the basis of slender hypotheses that the authorship of the verses in the Therīgāthā cannot be ascribed to the women who sang them. Be that as it may, there is no gainsaying of the fact, in the absence of any historical truth to the contrary, that in the Buddha's days, women who broke through the fetters of worldly life and gained the joys of asexual rational beings, sang extempore learned and thoughtful verses on

Instances of educated women.

many occasions—specially when Māra, the Buddhist Satan, tried, in vain, his level best to lead astray these saintly sisters sometimes by joyful or lewd temptations and sometimes by frightful sights. The gāthās sang by women and the record of the educational career of certain individual ladies mentioned below evince the fact that education must have been in vogue amongst females in the days of Gautama Buddha.

The Saṁyutta Nikāya refers to a woman who had the power of oratory. It says that Sukkā, a bhikkhuṇī, delivered a religious sermon to a big audience at Rājagaha. A yakkha being pleased with her declared in the streets of Rājagaha that Sukkā was distributing honey and those who were wise should go and drink it. (pt. I., pp. 212-213). Khemā mastered Vinaya well. (Dīpavaṁsa, Sec. XVIII). She was learned, intelligent, vastly read, eloquent and full of ready wit. King Pasenadi went to her, saluted her and questioned her whether a being after death is reborn or not Khemā replied, "It is not answered by the Blessed One." The king asked her the cause of the Buddha not answering this question. The bhikkhuṇī asked the king whether he had any body who could count the sand of the Ganges and drops of water in the sea; the king answered in the negative. The bhikkhuṇī said, "If any being is free from attachment of five Khandhas, it becomes immeasureable and fathomless like a big sea. Hence rebirth after death of such a being is beyond conception." The king was pleased with her for her answer and left her. (S. N. IV., 374-380). Bhaddā Kuṇḍalakesā, on renouncing the world, entered the order of the

Niganṭhas. She learnt the doctrine of the Niganṭhas and left their company and roaming hither and thither she used to go to learned persons and learnt their methods of knowledge. There was no one equal to her in debate except Sāriputta by whom she was defeated in argument. (Therīgāthā, commy. pp 99).

The Majjhima Nikāya speaks of Dhammadinnā, a learned woman well-versed in Buddhist philosophy. One day Dhammadinnā's husband asked her many questions about Sakkāyadiṭṭhi (belief in one's own body to be soul), Sakkāyanirodha, Ariya-aṭṭhangiko-maggo, Saṁkhāras, nirodhasamāpatti, manner of rising up from nirodhasamāpatti, and several kinds of Vedanā. Dhammadinnā gave satisfactory answers to each. She said, "Five upādānakhandhas constitute Sakkāya, tanhā means sakkāya samudayo, destruction of tanhā means sakkāya nirodha, the noble eight-fold path is the means of attaining Sakkāyanirodha. Ignorant people take the five upādāna khandhas jointly and separately as attā (soul). The learned noble disciples do not take them in this sense of speech, inhalation, exhalation and act of mind. Those who attain Nirodhasamāpatti are stopped one after another. The three kinds of Vedanā are sukha, dukkha and adukkhamasukha (Pt. I. pp. 299 foll). Dhammadinnā mastered Vinaya well. (Dīpavaṁsa, Sec XVIII).

The Vimānavatthu commentary records a single instance of an educated maid. It says that Latā, daughter of an upāsaka of Sāvatthi was learned, wise and intelligent. (p. 131). Saṅghamittā possessed the three-fold science. She knew well the magical powers. (Dīpavaṁsa, Sec. XV). So completely did she master the Vinaya Piṭaka that she was capable of teaching it to others. She taught Vinaya Piṭaka in Anurādhapura and the five collections (of the Sutta Piṭaka) and the seven Treatises (of the Abhidhamma) (Dīpavaṁsa, Sec. XVIII). Añjali possessed the six (supernatural) faculties and the great superhuman powers. She mastered the Vinayapiṭaka and like Saṅghamittā, she could teach it to others. She came to Anurādhapura along with sixteen thousand bhikkhuṇīs and taught Vinaya Piṭaka. Uttarā possessed three-fold science and knew well the magical powers. She was a well-read woman. She came to Anurādhapura in Ceylon. There she taught Vinaya Piṭaka, five collections of the Sutta Piṭaka and the seven Treatises of the Abhidhamma. Kāli was the daughter of a rogue. She was well-versed in the whole of the sacred scriptures and was of pure mind. She taught Vinayapiṭaka in Anurādhapura. Sapattā, Channā, Upāli and Revatī were the highest among the Vinaya studying bhikkhuṇīs. Sīvalā and Mahāruhā taught Vinaya piṭaka, the five collections of the Suttapiṭaka and the seven Treatises of the Abhidhamma in Anurādhapura. Samuddanāvā taught Vinaya piṭaka in Anurādhapura (Dīpavaṁsa, Sec. XVIII). Hemā possessed three-fold science and knew well the superhuman powers. (Dīpavaṁsa, Sec. XV). She taught Vinaya piṭaka, the five collections of the Suttapiṭaka and the seven Treatises of the Abhidhamma (Sec. XVIII). Aggimittā possessed three-fold science and knew well the super-human powers (Ibid, Sec. XV). Cūlanāgā, Dhannā, Soṇā Mahātissā, Cūlasumanā and Mahāsumanā were learned, illustrious and versed in the tradition (Ibid, Sec. XVIII). Nanduttarā was versed in Vijjā and Sippa (Therī. Commy. p. 87). Paṭācārā was the foremost of the bhikkhunīs who mastered Vinaya Piṭaka (A. N. I. 25; cf. Dīpavaṁsa, Sec. XVIII). Besides the therīs mentioned above there were others who were also distinguished for their learning. Uppalavaṇṇā, Sobhitā, Isidāsikā, Visākhā, Sabalā, Saṁghadāsī and Nandā mastered Vinaya well. Therī Uttarā, Mallā, Pabbatā Pheggu, Dhammadāsī, Aggimittā, and Pasādapāla taught Vinayapiṭaka the five collections of the Suttapiṭaka and the seven Treatises of the Abhidhamma in Anurādhapura, Sadhammanandi, Somā, Giriddhi, Dāsī and Dhammā were well-versed in the Vinaya; Sumanā, Mahilā, Mahādevī, Padumā, and Hemāsā taught Vinayapiṭaka in Anurādhapura. (Dīpavaṁsa, Sec. XVIII). The Divyāvadāna refers to female students reading Buddhavacana at night (p. 532).

CHAPTER VI

WOMEN AND BUDDHISM

Influence of Buddha's doctrine on women.

The Buddha's doctrine produced a marvelous effect on many women, rich or poor, married or unmarried, who were moved by the attractive power of the Buddha's dhamma and renounced the world to lead a pious life in the expectation of a happy rebirth or in order to annihilate rebirth altogether. We have already referred to a number of courtesans who led saintly lives after listening to the Buddha. Ladies of the Śākya family were naturally the earliest women to come under the influence of the new creed. The women appear to have enjoyed a greater amount of independence and free thinking among the Śākyas than among the peoples of the plains perhaps owing to the same scarcity of women that forced them to enact a law prohibiting multiple marriages. It is significant that the Śākya ladies were the first to come out of their hearth and home and embrace the hardy life of nuns in order to ensure the emancipation of their souls. The master who always evinced a solicitude for not violating the customs, was not willing to ordain them. But the importunities of the Śākya ladies prevailed at last, and the Master, though unwilling had to yield. Many females, dames, daughters-in-law and maidens of the clans heard of the great enlightenment of the Buddha, of the very truth of the Norm and of the excellent practices of the Order. They were highly pleased with the systems. Afraid of the round of rebirth, they sought permission of husbands, parents and kins and renounced the world. They received instructions from the Master and the elders and striving hard soon attained Arahatship. The Therīgāthā and its commentary tell us in what light the monastic life presented itself to women in the days of Gautama Buddha. It was, in some cases, the influence of the Buddha's doctrine, particularly the attractive power of the Buddha's dhamma, that exerted a force from behind and impelled women to renounce the world; while in others it was the strong motive for escaping from suffering, physical, mental, moral, domestic and social or for keeping oneself away from some intolerable circumstances despite all hindrances—duties to children, parents, husbands or masters. Many a bereaved mother, childless widow and penitent harlot were moved by the drawing power of the Buddha's dhamma and renounced the world to get themselves relieved from grief, reproach and repentance. The young girl to escape the humiliation of being sold to the suitor at the highest bid and the thoughtful woman to avoid the burden of conventional tradition on her intellectual development took to saintly life. The wife of a rich man realising the emptiness of an idle life of luxury renounced the world. The poor man's wife unable to bear the cares and anxieties of an impoverished family followed her rich sister. Thus freed from the fetters of worldly life these women used to lead the hard life of bhikkhunīs and therīs in the expectation of having after death a happier and more comfortable rebirth in some heaven or other. They were held in high esteem by bhikkhus, theras and laymen alike.

So deeply did the Buddha's dhamma strike a root into the holy minds of these pious women that

Māra, the Buddhist Satan and emblem of everything sinful, could not succeed in winning them over to his side after trying all sorts of temptations nor could profligates stir up sensual desires in these women who completely subdued their passions. An awful instance is furnished by the Therīgāthā commentary. Subhā, a bhikkhuṇī, after being established in the fruition of the third stage of sanctification, while walking along the Jīvaka's mango-grove, was seen by a profligate who blocked her path and wanted her to indulge in sensual pleasures with him. Subhā explained to him why she had renounced the world and asked him to let her go away. The debauchee heeded not. Then Subhā extracted one of her eyes and placed it on his hand. The profligate was astonished at this and begged pardon of her. Subhā left the place and came to the Master who gave her instructions. She developed insight and very soon attained arahatship with analytical knowledge. (Therīgāthā commentary, 245 foll).

Influence of Buddha's dhamma on household women.

Many other instances may be cited of the Buddha's benign influence on household women. Sumanā, sister of the king of Kośala, was a rājakumārī of Sāvatthī One day she went to the Buddha accompanied by five hundred chariots and five hundred princesses. She questioned the Buddha, "Will there be any difference between a dāyaka (charitable) pupil and an adāyaka (uncharitable) pupil of the Blessed One if they go to heaven after death?" The Buddha answered it in the affirmative. A dāyaka pupil would get a longer life, beauty, happiness, wealth and influence in heaven than an adāyaka pupil." Another question was put to the Buddha, "Will there be any difference between them if they fall from heaven and obtain human bodies again?" To this the following reply was given, "A dāyaka pupil would get a longer life, beauty, happiness, wealth and influence in this world than an adāyaka pupil." "Will there be any difference between them if both of them become bhikkhus?" It was answered thus, "A dāyaka pupil would get four requisities more than an adāyaka pupil without asking anything from any body." Sumanā further asked, "Will there be any difference if both of them become arahats?" Buddha answered in the negative. Sumanā said, "One should give charity as it is helpful in heaven, in the human world as well as in the life of a monk." The Buddha approved of what she said. (A. N., III., pp. 32-34). Thereafter one day Sumanā heard the Master preach the doctrine to King Pasenadi. She believed and was established in the Refuge and the Precepts. On her grandmother's death, Sumanā went to the Vihāra with the king. She heard the Master teach and entered the order. By virtue of the maturity of her knowledge she won arahantship, together with thorough knowledge of the Norm in form and in meaning. (Therīgāthā commentary, pp. 22-23; cf. A. N., III., 32-34).

Sujātā was born at Sāketa in a banker's family. One day she saw the Master, did obeisance and took a seat near him. The Master expounded the Norm in form and meaning. Then and there she attained Arahantship with paṭisambhidā. Saluting the Master she went home. There she secured permission of her husband and parents to renounce the world. She was admitted to the order of the bhikkhus. (Therī. Commy. 136-137).

Vaḍḍhamātā heard a bhikkhuṇī preach and became a believer. Her faith in the Buddha's dhamma grew so strong that she handed over her only child Vaḍḍha to her kinsman and herself renounced the world, came over to the bhikkhuṇīs and entered the order. Very soon she attained Arahantship. (Therī. Commy. 171-172).

Bhaddā was the daughter of a householder living in the town of Kimbila at Sāvatthī. She was married to Rohaka, son of another householder. Bhaddā was a maiden of good conduct, hence she was known as Bhaditthī, or the gentle dame. Once two chief disciples of the Buddha came to Kimbila and were invited by Rohaka. Bhaddā with her husband offered them good food and drink and various other things. She served them in every way and listened to their discourses. She embraced the faith and received the five sīlas. Since then Buddha used to observe the Uposatha on the 8th, 14th and 15th day of every half month. (Vimānavatthu commentary, 109-110).

The Dhammapada commentary records the incidents in the life of another Sujātā, daughter of the chief of Senānigāma near Uruvela. She offered rice gruel to the Buddha in the forenoon of the day in which Siddhattha became the Buddha. She was childless but she promised that she would worship the deity of a nigrodha tree on the bank of the river Nerañjarā. When a child was born to her, she came with rice gruel to offer to the deity but thinking the Buddha seated there to be the deity, she offered rice gruel to him. (D. C., I., 86).

Muttā was born of a poor brahmin named Oghāṭaka in the country of Kosala. She was married to a hunchbacked brahmin. She induced her husband to consent to her leaving the world. She practised self-control and exercised insight till she won Arahatship with Paṭisambhidā. (Therī. Commy. pp. 14-15).

A daughter-in-law of a certain family at Sāvatthī received an arahat with great delight. She offered some portion of the cakes which she had got for her own use. The Thera accepted the offering and went away blessing her. In consequence of the merit acquired she, after death, was reborn in the Tāvatiṁsa heaven, (Vimānavatthu Commy. p. 61).

The wife of a poor man named Puṇṇa, the servant of a banker of Rājagaha, was once bringing cooked rice for her husband who was then working in the field. On her way she met Sāriputta and gladly offered the whole of it. Sāriputta accepted the offering and blessed her. She returned home, cooked rice again and came to the field. She explained the cause of her delay. Puṇṇa was highly pleased with her, partook of the cooked rice and placing his head on his wife's lap fell asleep. When he woke up he found the cultivated field full of gold. He and his wife realised that they had received gold through the influence of the Thera Sāriputta. They took some gold to the king and related the whole matter to him. The king sent his men to take the gold but as soon as the gold was placed on the cart it turned into earth. The officers related this to the king who realised that the wealth being the reward for the good deeds of the poor family, could be enjoyed by them alone, and accordingly ordered his officers to take the gold on behalf of Puṇṇa. The gold was brought into the palace and piled up there. The king made Puṇṇa the nagarasetṭhi with the name Bahudhanasetṭhi. Puṇṇa made plentiful gifts to the Buddha and the congregation on the occasion of his being installed as setṭhi and his entrance into the new palace. Puṇṇa and his wife attained the first stage of sanctification by meritorious deeds. (Vimānavatthu commy. 62-74).

Suppiyā was a householder's wife at Benares. She was devoted to the Buddha, Dhamma and Saṁgha and always used to go to the vihāra to do whatever any bhikkhu liked. She used to look after every bhikkhu as to his health, etc. She used to prepare diet for sick bhikkhus. One day a bhikkhu took purgative and asked Suppiyā to prepare a kind of cooked meat suitable for him. She promised to supply but failed to get meat of any animal who met with a natural death. She fulfilled her promise by having the flesh of her thigh cooked for the bhikkhu. Her husband was surprised to hear of her strong devotion to the bhikkhu saṁgha. The Buddha was invited to her house and fed to his satisfaction. The Buddha enquired of Suppiyā and was informed that she was ill. She was brought before the Buddha with great difficulty. The Buddha blessed her for this exemplary sacrifice. He saw her wound which was cured instantly and she became all right. (Vinaya Piṭaka, 1., 216-219).

Female believers' place in a heretic family.

There lived in Rājagaha a wealthy householder whose wife and daughter-in-law were staunch believers in the Buddha. One day they started to worship the relics of the Buddha with sweet-scented flowers and perfumes, etc. The householder asked them not to go but they did not hear him. They worshipped the Buddha and returned home. Shortly afterwards they fell ill and died. They were reborn in Devaloka. (P. D. on the Petavattu (P. T. S.) pp. 212-215).

A certain woman of Sāvatthī was very faithful and obedient to her husband. She was truthful, charitable and an observer of precepts. She used to make offerings according to her means. After death she was reborn in the Tāvatiṁsa heaven (V. C. 56-57).

Uttarā was the daughter of Puṇṇa, a servant of a Banker of Rājagaha. Her husband, father-in-law and mother-in-law were false believers and she had no opportunity of making any gifts to the bhikkhus and the congregation. She informed her father of her difficulty. Puṇṇa sent a large sum of money to Uttarā who allowed her husband to spend a portion of it to enjoy the company of the courtezan named Sirimā for a fortnight and during this period she was freed from restraint and could offer charity to the Buddha and his disciples and listen to the Buddha's sermon. The Buddha with his disciples came there and held a religious discourse. Uttarā listened to it and attained the second stage of sanctification. Sirimā with five hundred gaṇikās who had thus an opportunity of hearing the discourses of the Master, attained the first stage.

Shortly afterwards Uttarā died and was reborn in the Tāvatiṁsa heaven. (V. C. 62-74; cf. Dhammapada commentary, III., p. 302 foll.).

There lived at Rājagaha, a girl of the family that supported Mahāmoggallāna. Daily she used to offer charities to the bhikkhus. When grown up she was married to a young man of a family of false believers. One day Mahāmoggallāna came and stood in front of her house. The girl invited him and offered him the cake which was reserved for her mother-in-law who when came to learn of it, grew angry and struck her on her shoulder. The girl died and after death was reborn in the Tāvatiṁsa heaven. (V. C. 120-121).

CHAPTER VII

BHIKKHUṆĪ-SAMGHA

According to all Buddhist accounts, Mahāpajāpati the Gotamī and five hundred Śākya ladies were the first to cut themselves off from the bondage of the world, and to institute the order of nuns. Mahāpajāpatī Gotamī, the foster-mother of the Buddha, though come of a royal family, was the first woman to sacrifice everything terrestrial, and to embrace the homeless life. She was the first to cut off her hair and to put on yellow robes. Thus we read—"Now at that time the Blessed Buddha was staying among the Śākyas in Kapilavatthu, in the Nigrodhārāma. And Mahāpajāpatī the Gotamī went to the place where the Blessed One was, and on arriving there, bowed down before the Blessed One, and remained standing on one side. And so standing she spoke thus to the Blessed One, 'It would be well, Lord, if women should be allowed to renounce their homes and enter the homeless state under the doctrine and discipline proclaimed by the Tathāgatha'. 'Enough, O Gotami! Let it not please thee that women should be allowed to do so!' (And a second and a third time did Mahāpajāpatī the Gotamī make the same request in the same words, and receive the same reply.) Then Mahāpajāpatī the Gotamī sad and sorrowful for that the Blessed One would not permit women to enter the homeless state, bowed down before the Blessed One, and keeping him on her right hand as she passed him, departed thence weeping and in tears.

Origin of the Bhikkhuṇi Samgha.

Now when the Blessed One had remained at Kapilavatthu as long as he thought fit, he set out on his journey towards Vesāli; and travelling straight on, he in due course arrived thereat. And there at Vesāli the Blessed One stayed, in the Mahāvana, in the Kuṭāgāra Hall.

And Mahāpajāpatī the Gotamī cut off her hair, and put on orange-coloured robes, and set out with a number of women of the Śākya clan, towards Vesāli, and in due course she arrived at Vesāli, at the Mahāvana at the Kuṭāgāra Hall. And Mahāpajāpatī the Gotamī, with swollen feet and covered with dust, sad and sorrowful, weeping and in tears, took her stand outside under the entrance porch.

And the Venerable Ānanda saw her so standing there, and on seeing her so he said to Mahāpajāpātī, 'Why standest thou there, outside the porch, with swollen feet and covered with dust, sad and sorrowful, weeping and in tears?' 'Inasmuch, O Ānanda, as the Lord, the Blesssed One, does not permit women to renounce their homes and enter the homeless state under the doctrine and discipline proclaimed by the Tathāgatha.'

Then did the Venerable Ānanda go up to the place where the Blessed One was, and bow down before the Blessed One, and take his seat on one side. And, so sitting, the Venerable Ānanda said to the Blessed One: 'Behold, Lord, Mahāpajāpatī the Gotamī is standing outside under the entrance porch, with swollen feet and covered with dust, sad and sorrowful, weeping and in tears, inasmuch as the Blessed One does not permit women to renounce their homes and enter the homeless state under the doctrine and discipline proclaimed by the Blessed One. It were well, Lord, if women were to have permission granted to them to do so as she desires.' 'Enough Ānanda! let it not please that women should be allowed to do so! (and a second and a third did Ānanda make the same request, in the same words, and receive the same reply.)

Then the venerable Ānanda thought: 'The Blessed One does not give his permission, let me now ask, the Blessed One on another ground.' And the venerable Ānanda said to the Blessed One: 'are women, Lord, capable—when they have gone forth from the household life and entered the homeless state, under the doctrine and discipline proclaimed by the Blessed One—are they capable of realising the fruit of conversation, or of the second Path, or of the third Path or of Arahatship?' 'They are capable Ānanda!' 'If then, Lord they are capable thereof, since Mahāpajāpatī the Gotamī has proved herself of great service to the Blessed One, when as aunt and nurse she nourished him and gave him milk, and on the death of his mother suckled the Blessed One at her own breast; it were well, Lord that women should have permission to go forth from the household life and enter the homeless state, under the doctrine and discipline proclaimed by the Tathāgata.'

'If then, Ānanda, Mahāpajāpatī the Gotamī take upon herself the Eight Chief Rules, let that be reckoned to her as her initiation.'

Then the Venerable Ānanda, when he had learnt from the Blessed One these Eight Chief Rules, went to Mahāpajāpatī the Gotamī and told her all that the Blesssed One had said.

'Just Ānanda, as a man or a woman, when young and of tender years, accustomed to adorn himself, would, when he had bathed his head, receive with both hands a garland of lotus flowers, or of jasmine flowers or of atimuttaka flowers, and place it on the top of his head; even so do I, Ānanda, take upon me these eight chief Rules, never to be transgressed my life long.'

Then the venerable Ānanda returned to the Blessed One, and bowed down before him, and took his seat, on one side. And, so sitting, the venerable Ānanda said to the Blessed One; 'Mahāpajāpatī the Gotamī, Lord, has taken upon herself the Eight Chief Rules, the aunt of the Blessed One has received the upasampadā initiation.' (Vinaya Texts, S. B. E., Vol. XX., pt. III., pp. 320, et seq; Cf. Manorathapūraṇi, Sinhalese Ed., 203).

Now Mahāpajāpatī received ordination, and 500 Śākya ladies who followed her were also ordained at the same time. Thus ordained great Pajāpatī came before the Master, and saluting him, stood on one side. The Blessed One taught her the Norm. She took up under him the system of exercise and soon after obtained Arahantship accompanied by initiative and analytical knowledge. The other five hundred bhikkhuṇīs, at the end of Nandaka's sermon (Majjhima Nikāya, III, pp. 270 ff) became endowed with the six branches of initiative knowledge. (cf. Therīgāthā Commentary, pp. 140 foll).

Besides the 500 Śākya ladies, some members of the Bodhisatta's harem, viz, Tissā, two Dhirās, Mittā, Bhaddā and Upasamā renounced the world along with Mahāpajāpatī Gotamī and in due course obtained Arahantship (Th. Commy. 12-13).

Bhaddā Kaccānā came of the family of a Śākya named Suppabuddha. She was so named because her skin was like gold (kāñcana). When grown up she was married to Gautama Buddha. Afterwards she bore a son who was named Rāhula. On the birthday of this child Gautama renounced the world and after attaining Bodhi he came back to Kapilavatthu and preached his doctrine to his clansmen. On the death of the great king, Suddhodana, she went to Mahāpajāpatī Gotamī and entered the Order. Since then she came to be known as Bhaddā Kaccānā. In course of time she reached the fulness of spiritual insight and attained Arahantship. She was assigned a chief place among the Bhikkhuṇīs possessing great supernatural powers. (Manorathapūraṇī, pp. 224-225; cf. A. N., I., p. 25).

After Mahāpajāpatī the Gotamī and several other Śākya ladies had received ordination, the Order of Bhikkhuṇīs was well established and multiplied in diverse villages, towns and country districts.

Bhikkhuṇīs and therīs were exempted from all sorts of punishment for any offence committed before entering the order. Once a Licchavi wife committed adultery. Her husband resolved to kill her, so she went to Sāvatthī and succeeded in getting herself ordained by a bhikkhuṇī. Her husband came to Sāvatthī, saw her ordained and complained to king

Pasenadi of Kosala. He also informed the king that his wife had become a bhikkhuṇī. The king said that as she had become a bhikkhuṇī, no punishment could be inflicted on her. (Bhikkhuṇīvibhaṅga, Saṅghādisesa, Vol. II., p. 225). The punishment for a woman who dishonoured the bed of her husband was so severe that the husband could with impunity take away her life. But even an adulterous woman could save herself from punishment by entering the congregation of nuns by getting the pabbajjā ordination. (Vinaya Piṭaka by H. Oldenberg, Vol. IV. pp. 225-226).

Conditions for entering the Order.

There were eight conditions on which a woman could enter the Order. The conditions are as follows:—

(1) A bhikkhuṇī even if she is 100 years old should worship a new bhikkhu.

(2) A bhikkhuṇī must not spend the lent before the dwelling place of a bhikkhu.

(3) A bhikkhuṇī must go twice in a month to take instructions from a bhikkhu.

(4) After the expiry of the lent, a bhikkhuṇī should ask pardon for any fault, seen, heard or thought of from both the bhikkhu and the bhikkhuṇīsaṁgha.

(5) A bhikkhunī should ask pardon from both the saṁghas if any serious offence is committed.

(6) A bhikkhuṇī should ask for upasampadā from both the saṁghas after she has learnt six precepts for two years.

(7) A bhikkhuṇī must not abuse or speak ill of any bhikkhu.

(8) A bhikkhuṇī must not talk with a bhikkhu but a bhikkhu can give instructions to a bhikkhuṇī (Vinaya Piṭaka Vol. II. pp. 253-255).

The rules for the guidance of a bhikkhuṇīsaṁgha.

The bhikkhuṇī saṁgha has several rules which the bhikkhuṇīs are required to obey. The rules, as will be evident from their character, are very strict. They are as follows :—

(1) A bhikkuṇī must not collect more than one alms bowl in a vihāra.

(2) A thing asked for by a bhikkhuṇī from any upāsaka or upāsikā cannot be taken in exchange for another thing.

(3) The thing given to a bhikkhuṇī for a purpose must be used by her for that purpose only.

(4) A bhikkhuṇī cannot ask for anything, the value of which is more than 16 kahāpaṇas from any person although she is requested by the person to ask for something from him.

(5) A bhikkhuṇī must not take any white onion.

(6) A bhikkhuṇī must not accept paddy.

(7) A bhikkhuṇī should not throw impurities on the road through the window and also on the field.

(8) A bhikkhuṇī should not attend to dancing, singing and other instrumental music.

(9) A bhikkhuṇī should not talk with any person alone in the dark.

(10) She should sit and talk with any man in a covered place.

(11) She should not do so even in moonlight by sitting on the meadow when there are no other persons.

(12) She should not talk with any man alone in the public street or cross roads where there are crows.

(13) She should not go away from the house where she gets her food daily without taking permission from the head of the house.

(14) She should not sit or lie down in a house where she enters in the afternoon without taking permission from the head of the house.

(15) She cannot curse anybody.

(16) She cannot take her bath being naked.

(17) Two bhikkhuṇīs cannot lie on the same bed and cannot cover their bodies with the same covering.

(18) If a bhikkhuṇī fall ill, the companion bhikkhuṇī should nurse her or cause her to be nursed by others.

(19) A bhikkhuṇī should not drive out or cause to be driven out another bhikkhuṇī to whom she has given shelter.

(20) She should not associate herself with a householder or householder's son.

(21) She should walk about with weapons within her own country in times of fear of robbers, dacoits, and other wicked persons.

(22) During the lent she must not travel from place to place.

(23) After lent she must not stay in the vihāra.

(24) A bhikkhuṇī must not go to see a palace, royal-garden, picture-gallery, pleasure garden, garden, tank having beautiful flowers, etc.

(25) She must not enjoy a valuable couch or a beautiful bedstead.

(26) She must not serve a householder.

(27) She must not give food with her own hands to a householder, a paribbājaka or a paribbājikā.

(28) She must not leave her dwelling place without placing it in charge of any other bhikkhuṇī.

(29) She must not learn any art for her livelihood

(30) She must not teach any art to anybody.

(31) She must not enter any hermitage where a bhikkhu dwells without his permission.

(32) She must not abuse a bhikkhu.

(33) She must not take food beforehand when invited to take food in another's place.

(34) She must not be attached to any particular family.

(35) She must not spend the lent in a hermitage having no bhikkhu.

(36) A bhikkhuṇī must go to take instructions from a bhikkhu.

(37) She must not make any female her disciple who has not received her parents' consent to give up household life.

(38) She must not go in a conveyance when fit.

(39) She must not put on ornaments and take her bath in perfumed water.

(40) She must not take her seat in the presence of a bhikkhu without his permission.

(41) She must not put any question without taking the bhikkhu's permission.

(42) She is prohibited from going out alone at night. (Vinaya Piṭaka.)

(43) Bhikkhuṇīs should receive instructions from the bhikkhus by turn (M. N. III. 270). They should learn the precepts common to the bhikkhus and bhikkhuṇīs and the precepts especially meant for the bhikkhuṇīs should be learnt by the bhikkhuṇīs (Vinayapiṭaka, II., p. 258).

(44) The bhikkhuṇīs should not wilfully touch the bodies of laymen (Vinayapiṭaka, IV., pp. 220-221). They are also prohibited to touch the bodies of the bhikkhus with lustful thoughts (Ibid, p. 211).

(45) In all assemblies where there is a sāmaneri or a bhikkhuṇī, the pātimokkha should not be recited and also in the Pavāraṇā ceremony (V. P., Vol., I. p. 130 & Vol. I p. 167).

(46) The bhikkhuṇīs should not live in forests because they might meet with. dangers as in the case of Uppalavaṇṇā (D. C. Vol. II. pp. 48-51). The Vinaya Piṭaka informs us that a robe once given to a bhikkhuṇī should not be taken back (Vol. IV. p. 247).

The bhikkhuṇīs should not be saluted and honoured by the bhikkhus. (V. P. II. 257-258).

The bhikkhuṇīs should not help a bhikkhuṇī who is excommunicated by the Saṁgha.

Violation of orders.

A bhikkhuṇī who knowingly hides any pārājikā offence of any other bhikkhuṇī, is also guilty of pārājikā.

If a bhikkhuṇī follows a bhikkhu excommunicated by the bhikkhusaṁgha, will be guilty of pārājikā.

A bhikkhuṇī cannot bring any suit against any householder, or householder's son, slave, employee even samaṇa or paribbājaka. If she does so, she will be guilty of saṁghādidesa offence.

If a person with evil motive sends presents to any bhikkhuṇī and if she knowingly accepts them, the bhikkhuṇī will be guilty of saṁghādidesa offence.

Buddha's prediction on the effect of the admittance of women into the Order.

"If Ānanda, women had not received permission to go out from the household life and enter the homeless state, under the doctrine and discipline proclaimed by the Tathāgata, then would the pure religion, Ānanda, have lasted long, the good law would have stood fast for a thousand years. But since, Ānanda, women have now received that permission, the pure religion, Ānanda, will not now last long, the good law will now stand fast for only five hundred years. Just, Ānanda, as houses in which there are many women and but few men are easily violated by robber burglars, just so Ānanda under whatever doctrine and discipline women are allowed to go out from the household life into the homeless state, the religion will not last long. And just, Ānanda, as when the disease called mildew falls upon a field of rice in fine condition, that field of rice does not continue long; just so, Ānanda, under whatsoever doctrine and discipline women are allowed to go forth from the household life into the homeless state, that religion will not last long. And just Ānanda, as when the disease called blight falls upon a field of sugarcane in good condition, that field of sugarcane does not continue long, just so, Ānanda, under whatsoever doctrine and discipline women are allowed to go forth from the household life into the homeless state, that religion does not last long. And just, Ānanda, as a man would in anticipation build an embankment to a great reservoir, beyond which the water should not overpass; just even so, Ānanda, have I in anticipation laid down these eight chief rules for the bhikkhus, their life long not to be overpassed. (Vinaya Texts, S. B. E , Pt. III., pp. 325-326).

Buddha's prediction was fulfilled when many troubles arose on account of the frequent meetings between the bhikkhus and the bhikkhuṇīs and the bhikkhuṇīs and the lay people as we find in the case of Thullanandā and Dabba the mallian and also Abhirūpanandā and Sālho, grandson of Migāra, the banker of Sāvatthī. (Vinaya Piṭaka, IV., pp. 201 foll).

CHAPTER VIII

PROMINENT BUDDHIST WOMEN

We shall conclude our monograph with an account of some famous women who figure prominently in the early Buddhist texts. The account will show, if any further proof be needed, that women were not a negligible factor in the ancient Buddhist community of India.

Abhirūpanandā.

Abhirūpanandā was the daughter of Khemaka, the Śākya. She was called Nandā the Fair for her great beauty and amiability. Her beloved kinsman, Carabhuta, died on the day on which she was to choose him from amongst her suitors. She had to leave the world against her will. Though she entered the order, she could not forget that she was beautiful. Fearing that the Buddha would rebuke her, she used to avoid his presence. The Buddha knew that the time had come for her to acquire knowledge and asked Mahāpajāpatī Gotamī to bring all the bhikkhuṇīs before him to receive instructions. Nandā sent a proxy for her. The Buddha said, "Let no one come by proxy." So she was compelled to come to him. The Buddha by his supernatural power conjured up a beautiful woman who became transferred into an old and fading figure. It had the desired effect and she became an Arahant. (Therīgāthā commentary, 25-26).

Jentī.

Jentī or Jentā was born in a princely family of the Licchavīs at Vaiśālī. She won Arahantship after hearing the Dhamma preached by the Buddha. She developed the seven Sambojjhaṅgas. (Ibid. p. 27).

Cittā was born at Rājagaha in the family of a leading burgess. When she was of age, she one day heard the Master preach and believed in his doctrine. She was ordained by Mahāpajāpati the Gotamī. In her old age she climbed the Vulture's peak and lived like a recluse. Her insight expanded and she won Arahantship (Therīgāthā commentary, p. 33).

Cittā.

Sukkā was born at Rājagaha in the family of a rich householder. When she attained years of discretion, she believed in the Master's teaching and became a lay disciple. One day she heard Dhammadinnā preach and was so greatly moved that she renounced the world and followed Dhammadinnā. She performed all the exercises for her insight and very soon attained Arahantship with paṭisambhidā. Thereupon she became a great preacher and was attended by five hundred bhikkhus. One day along with the other bhikkhunīs she went to the hermitage of the bhikkhunīs and taught the Buddha's doctrine in such a way that every body listened to her with rapt attention; even the tree-spirit was so much moved that it began to praise her. At this the people were excited, came to the sister and listened to her attentively (Therīgāthā commentary, 57-61).

Sukkā.

Selā was born in the kingdom of Ālavī, as the king's daughter. She was also known as Ālavikā. One day while yet a maid she went with the king and heard the Master preach. She became a believer and lay disciple. A few days after she took orders

Selā.

and performed the exercises for insight. She subjugated the complexities of thought, word and deed and soon won Arahantship. Thereafter she lived at Sāvatthī when the Buddha was there. She entered Andhavana to meditate after finishing midday meal. Māra once tried in vain to seduce her to choose the sensuous life. (Th. commy, 61 foll, cf. S. N. pt. I., p. 128).

Sīhā.

Sīhā was born at Vesālī as the daughter of General Sīha's sister. She was named after her maternal uncle. When she grew up, she heard the Master teaching the Norm to her maternal uncle and became a believer. She was permitted by her parents to enter the Order. For seven years she could not acquire insight as her mind was always inclined towards objects of external charm. Then she intended to die. She took a noose, hung it round the bough of a tree and fastened it round her neck. Thus she succeeded in impelling her mind to insight which grew within and she won Arahantship. She then took off the rope from her neck and went back to her hermitage. (Th. commy. pp. 79-80).

Sundarī Nandā.

Sundarī Nandā was born in the royal family of the Śākyas. She was known as the beautiful Nandā. Thinking about the fact that her elder brother, her mother, her brother, her sister and her nephew had renounced the world, she too left it. Even after her renunciation, she was obsessed with the idea of her beauty and would not approach the Lord lest she should be reproached for her folly. The Lord taught her in the same way as he did in the case of Nandā, the Fair. She listened to the Master's teachings and enjoyed the benefit of the fruition of the first stage of sanctification. He then instructed her saying, "Nandā, there is in this body not even the smallest essence. It is but a heap of bones covered with flesh and besmeared with blood under the shadow of decay and death." Afterwards she became an Arahant. (Th. Commy. pp. 80 foll. cf. Manorathapūraṇī. pp. 217-218).

Khemā.

Khemā was born in the royal family of Sāgala. She was very beautiful and her skin was like gold. She became the consort of Bimbisāra. One day she heard that the Buddha was in the habit of speaking ill of beauty. Since then she did not appear before Buddha. The king was a chief supporter of the Buddha. He asked his court-poets to compose a song on the glories of the Veluvana hermitage and to sing the song so loudly that the queen might hear it. The royal order was carried out. Khemā heard of the beauty of the hermitage and with the king's consent she came to the Veluvana vihāra where the Buddha was staying at this time. When she was led before the Buddha, the latter conjured up a woman like a celestial nymph stood fanning him with a palm leaf. Khemā observed this woman to be more beautiful than she and was ashamed of her own grace. Sometime after she noticed again that the woman passed from youth to middle age and then to old age till with broken teeth, grey hair, and wrinckled skin, she fell on earth with her palm leaf. Then thought Khemā that her beautiful body would meet with the same fate as that of the nymph. Then the Master knew her thoughts and said that persons subject to lust suffer from the result of their action, while those freed from all bondage forsake the world. When the Master had finished speaking, Khemā, according to the commentary, attained Arahantship, and according to the Apadāna, she was established in the fruition of the first stage of sanctification and with the king's permission she entered the order before she became an Arahant. Thereafter she made a name for her insight and was ranked foremost amongst the bhikkhuṇīs possessing great wisdom. In vain Māra tried to tempt her with sensuous ideas. (Th. Commy, pp. 126, foll.; cf. Manorathapūraṇī, p. 205 cf. Aṅguttara N. I. p. 25).

Anopamā.

Anopamā was the daughter of a banker named Majjha living in Sāketa. She was of unique beauty. She was sued by many sons of bankers, higher officers of the state but she thought that there was no happiness in household life. She went to the Master and heard his teachings. Her intelligence matured. She strove hard for insight and was established in the third fruition. On the seventh day thereafter she attained Arahantship. (Th. Commy. 138-139).

Rohiṇī.

Rohiṇī was born at Vesālī in the house of a very prosperous brahmin. When grown up she went to the Master and heard him preach the doctrine. She obtained Satāpattiphalam. She converted her parents to Buddha's faith and with their permission entered the order. She performed the exercises for insight and very soon attained Arahantship. (Th. Commy. pp. 214. foll).

Subhā. Subhā was the daughter of a certain goldsmith of Rājagaha. She was very beautiful and was therefore called Subhā. When grown up she saw the Master and believed in his doctrine. The Master saw the maturity of her moral faculties and taught her the dhamma. She was afterwards established in the fruition of the first stage of sanctification. Thereafter she entered the Order under Mahāpajāpatī Gotamī. She strove hard for insight and in course of time she won Arahantship. (Th. commy. pp. 236 foll).

Tissā. Tissā was born at Kapilavastu among the Śākyas. She renounced the world with Mahāpajāpatī Gotamī and became spiritually so developed that she attained Arahatship. (Th. Commy. p 11).

Sumedhā. Sumedhā, daughter of King Koñca of Mantāvatī was averse to the pleasures of senses from her childhood. She renounced the world hearing the doctrine of the Buddha from the bhikkhuṇīs. Very soon she acquired insight and attained Arahatship. (Th. Commy. 272).

Visākhā. Visākhā was the daughter of Śumanādevī, wife of Dhanañjaya seṭṭhi, son of Meṇḍakaseṭṭhi. Her abode was at Bhaddiyanagara in the kingdom of Aṅga. When she was seven years old, Buddha with the Bhikkhusaṁgha went to the Bhaddiyanagara. Sumanādevī was one of the advisers of the king. Visākhā with 500 female companions and 500 chariots went to receive the Buddha who gave instructions to her according to her nature and she obtained Sotāpattiphalam. The Buddha was invited in Visākhā's house. Visākhā who was endowed with five kinds of beauty was married to Puṇṇavaddhana of Sāvatthī. The presents sent by the citizens of Sāvatthī for her were distributed by her among the citizens with great courtesy. She made the citizens her own relatives. She refused to salute the naked heretics who were worshipped by her father-in-law. The latter was converted into Buddhism through her efforts. Once Visākhā invited the Bhikkhus, and her father-in-law hearing the sermon obtained Sotāpattiphalam. (D. C. I. 384 foll). On the death of her grand-child who was very dear to her, Visākhā went to see the Buddha with wet cloth and wet hair. The Buddha asked her whether she would be satisfied if all the people of Sāvatthī be her sons and grandsons. She replied in the affirmative. The master asked her as to how many people met with their death at Sāvatthī. Visākhā said, "From one to ten." The Buddha told her, "Just think whether you would be free from wet cloth and wet hair." Visākhā said that she did not want so many sons and grandsons because acquisition of more sons and grandsons would bring great suffering. (Udāna 91-92). Visākhā, mother of Migāra, was the foremost of the charitable female devotees of the Buddha (A. N. I. p. 26). Once a sabbath day she went to the Buddha while the latter was in her palace named Pubbārāma. Buddha instructed Visākhā, "There was three kinds of uposatha and the ariya uposatha is the best of the uposathas. The Master then said that in order to observe Ariya uposatha one should meditate on the Buddha, Dhamma and Saṁgha. Sīlas must be unbroken and fully observed. One should also meditate on the qualities of gods. One should follow arahats who follow precepts throughout their lives. By observing Ariya uposatha one may obtain great happiness and may be reborn in one of the heavens commencing from the Cātummahārājika to Paranimmitavasavattī gods and enjoy great celestial happiness there (A. N. I. 205-215). Visākhā was further instructed by the Buddha, thus "Dependence on others is suffering, independence brings happiness. (Udāna p. 18). Visākhā once blamed the bhikkhus for not allowing her grandson to be ordained during the lent and owing to this delay her grandson's mind was changed. (Vinaya Piṭaka, I. 153). Once she went to the Buddha and invited him together with the bhikkhus to take food at her house the next morning. Heavy rains poured in the following morning and the bhikkhus being naked bathed themselves as they had no bathing costumes. Visākhā came to know this fact from her maid-servant who was sent for the bhikkhus. The Buddha together with the bhikkhus came to her house. She fed the Buddha and the Bhikkhus satisfactorily. After they had finished their meal, Visākhā prayed to the Buddha for the following boons:— As long as she would live, she would give garments for the rainy season to the bhikkhus, food to the guests and food to those going abroad, diet to the sick bhikkhus, food to the sick nurses, medicine to the sick bhikkhus, rice-gruel to the bhikkhus daily and bathing garments to the bhikkhuṇīs (V. P. Vol. I.

pp. 290-292). From this fact it is evident that Visākhā introduced bathing garments for the bhikkhuṇīs. It was Visākhā who offered a napkin to the Buddha which he accepted. (V. P. I. 296). We are further informed that Visākhā, as soon as she heard of the advent of the quarrelsome Kosambian bhikkhus, approached the Buddha to take his advice as to how she should deal with them. The Buddha advised her to offer charities to the two parties of the quarrelsome Kosambian monks. (V. P. I. 356). Visākhā prepared a golden waterpot for the Buddha. A sāmanera named Sumana brought water in that pot for the Buddha from the Anotatta lake. (D. C. IV. p. 135). Visākhā offered a waterpot and a broom to the Buddha which he accepted and also instructed the bhikkhus to use them. Once she went to the Buddha and offered a palm-leaf fan which he accepted. (V. P. II. 129-130). Visākhā was so very kind to the bhikkhus that she built a mansion for them who at first hesitated to use it but afterwards asked for Buddha's permission which was granted (V. P. II. 169). Visākhā went to see the hermitage of Khadiravaniyarevata but she found it to be in the midst of thorns and unfit for human habitation. (D. C. II. 188-200). She was an important personage because among the bhikkhus if there be any matter to be referred to, it was referred to her as we find in the case of Kuṇḍadhāna thera who with a woman at his back used to walk about (D. C. III. 54-55). In the family of Visākhā young girls used to serve the bhikkhus by making arrangements for their food, etc. (D. C. III. 161). Visākhā's son's daughter named Dattā who was entrusted to take care and serve Bhikkhusaṁgha in her absence, died. Visākhā was much afflicted with grief. The Buddha consoled her. (D. C. III. pp. 278-279). Visākhā was one day going to the city garden wearing all sorts of rich ornaments amongst which may be mentioned Mahālatā, an ornament of extraordinary beauty and of immense value. (cf. Dhammapada Commy. I, 412). On the way she thought why she was going to the city garden like a mere girl; it was better that she should go to the vihāra and listen to the discourses of the Buddha. Moved by the thought, she went to the Lord, put off her ornament, Mahālatā, and gave it to her maid-servant to keep it and to return it when she would come out of the vihāra. Thereafter she listned to the noble discourses of the Buddha. On coming out of the vihāra, she asked for her ornament. The maid-servant said that she had left it in the vihāra. Both of them returned to the vihāra and found it. Visākhā offered it to the Lord and under his directions built a vihāra with the sale-proceeds of the ornament which amounted to nine crores and a lac. Visākhā offered to her maid-servant all the merit that accrued for constructing the vihāra. The latter approved of her charity and died shortly afterwards. (Vimānavatthu commy. pp. 187-189).

Anulā.

Anulā was the queen of the king of Ceylon. Surrounded by five hundred girls she bowed to the theras and honoured them to her heart's content. Thera Mahinda preached Dhamma to them. Peta stories, vimāna stories and saccasamyutta were narrated to them. When they heard the most excellent portion of the doctrine, princess Anulā and her five hundred attendants attained Sotāpatti. She became a believer in the Buddha, Dhamma and Saṁgha. With her five hundred attendants she received the Pabbajjā ordination from Saṅghamittā Mahātherī. (Dīpavaṁsa, pp. 68 & 88; cf. Mahāvaṁsa, Geiger's Text, 108 & 155).

Gopikā. Gopikā was a Śākya princess. She was pleased with the Buddha, Dhamma and Saṁgha. She used to observe precepts fully, became disgusted with woman life and meditated to become a man. (Dīgha Nikāya, II., 271).

Candā. Candā came of a brahmin family. She earned her living by begging from door to door. One day she came to the spot where Paṭācārā had just finished her meal. The bhikkhuṇīs saw her hungry and gave her some food to eat. She ate the food and took her seat on one side. She then listened to the discourses of Therī Paṭācārā and renounced the world. She practised hard for insight. Her knowledge matured and her determination was strong. Hence she succeeded in attaining Arahatship with paṭisambhidā. (Th. commy. 120-121).

Guttā. Guttā came of a brahmin family at Sāvatthī. In her youth, household life became repugnant to her. She obtained her parent's consent and entered the Order under Mahāpajāpatī Gotamī. Thereafter she could not for sometime control her mind from external interests. Then the Master gave her suitable instructions and she attained Arahatship together with paṭisambhidā. (Th. Commy. pp. 157-159).

Vijayā.

Vijayā came of a certain clansman's family of Rājagaha. She was a friend of Khemā, when she heard that Khemā, a king's consort, had renounced the world, she went to Khemā who taught her the Norm and ordained her. Very soon she won insight and after a short time attained Arahatship with analytical knowledge. (Th. Commy. 159-160). Māra came to tempt her by saying, "You are young and beatiful, I am also young and beautiful, let us enjoy ourselves with music." She replied, "I find delight in rūpa, sadda, gandha, etc., and I don't like soft touch. I hate very much rotten body which is easily destructible. My ignorance is dispelled." Then Māra left her. (Saṁyutta Nikāya, I., 130-131).

Cālā, Upacālā and Sisupacālā.

Cālā, Upacālā and Sisupacālā were born in Magadha at the village of Nālaka as the children of a brahmaṇī named Surūpasārī. They were younger sisters of Sāriputta. When they heard that their brother had left the world for the Order, they too renounced the world and striving hard attained Arahatship. In vain Māra tried to stir up sensual desires in them. (Th. Commy. 162-163; cf. S. N. Pt. I., pp. 132-134).

Uppalavannā.

Uppalavannā came of a banker's family at Sāvatthī. Her skin was of the colour of the heart (*gabbha*) of the blue lotus. Hence she was called Uppalavaṇṇā. (cf. Samantapāsādikā, I., 272-273). Many princes and bankers' sons wanted to marry her. But she renounced the world, went to the bhikkhuṇīs and was ordained. Thereafter one day she lighted a lamp and by continually contemplating on the flame of the lamp she gradually obtained Arahatship with abhiññā and paṭisambhidā. (Th. Commy. 182, ff.) She was assigned a chief place among those who had the gift of Iddhi. (Manorathapūraṇī, p. 356; Aṅguttara Nikāya, I., 25). The Saṁyutta Nikāya tells us that Therī Uppalavaṇṇā went to Andhavana to meditate. There she sat at the foot of a sāla tree. Māra came to her and said to her, "You are sitting at the foot of a fully blossomed sāla tree, are you not afraid of the wicked?" She replied, "I do not care the wicked, I do not care you?" Māra left her. (pt. I., 131-132). After defeating Māra, Uppalavaṇṇā was molested by her maternal uncle's son, Ānanda, who was enamoured of her beauty and who wanted to marry her. Although Uppalavaṇṇā had become a bhikkhunī, Ānanda could not give up the desire of marrying her. Once Ānanda concealed himself in the room of the Therī under her bedstead in her absence. When the Therī returned home and lay herself down on the bedstead, Ānanda suddenly came out and committed rape on her. The therī informed the bhikkhuṇīs of this fact who through the bhikkhus brought this to the notice of the Buddha who prohibited the bhikkhuṇīs from living in forests. (D. C II. 48-51). Uppalavaṇṇā therī acquired the power of performing a miracle by coming to the presence of the Buddha to worship the Buddha with the pomp and grandeur of an individual monarch being surrounded by a retinue extending over 36,000 yojanas and this miracle was visible to an assembly extending over 12 yojanas (D. C. III. p. 211).

Sumaṅgalamātā. Sumaṅgalamātā came of a poor family at Sāvatthī. She was married to a basket-maker. She acquired great merit. One day while reflecting on all she had suffered as a lay-woman, she was much affected and her insight quickening, she attained Arahatship with analytical knowledge. (Th. Commy. 28-30).

Puṇṇā. Puṇṇā or Puṇṇikā acquired great merits in her previous birth but owing to her pride she could not root out kilesas (sins). She was born of a domestic slave at Sāvatthī in the household of Anāthapiṇḍika, the banker. She obtained Sotāpattiphalam after hearing the Sihanāda Suttanta. Afterwards Anāthapiṇḍika gave her freedom because she defeated a brahmin named Udakasuddhika. Puṇṇā renounced worldly life and entered the Order. She practised insight and very soon attained Arahatship with paṭisambhidā (Th. Commy. pp. 199 foll).

Sundarī. Sundarī was born at Benares as the daughter of Sujāta, a brahmin. On her brother's death, her father became overwhelmed with grief. With the advise of Therī Vāsiṭṭhī her father renounced the world, met the Buddha at Mithilā, entered the Order and in course of time attained Arahatship. Sundarī heard of her father's renouncing the world. She sacrificed all her wealth and pleasures of all kinds. She secured her mother's consent to leave the world. She then entered the Order and striving hard she attained Arahatship with paṭisambhidā (Th. Commy. 228 foll).

Vimalā.

Vimalā was born at Vesālī as the daughter of a public woman. When advanced in years she was moved to see one day the Venerable Mahāmoggallāna going about for alms. She went to his house to entice him. Mahāmoggallāna rebuked her. She was ashamed and became a believer and lay sister. Sometime after she entered the Order and very soon attained Arahatship. (Th. Commy. 76-77).

Mittākālikā.

Mittākālikā came of a brahmin's family at the town of Kammāssadammā in the kingdom of the Kurus. When she grew up she one day heard the teaching of the Great Discourse on the Mahāsatipaṭṭhāna and entered the Order of Sisters. For seven years she could not elevate herself intellectually. Later on she won Arahatship together with the analytical knowledge (Th. Commy. pp. 89-90).

Sakulā (Pakulā.)

Sakulā (Pakulā) was born in a brahmin family at Sāvatthī. Seeing the Master accepting the gift of the Jeta Grove, she became a believer. One day she heard the preaching of an arahat and was greatly convinced. She entered the Order, strove hard for insight and soon won Arahatship. She was given the foremost place by the Master among the bhikkhuṇīs possessing divine eyes. (Th. Commy. pp. 91 foll, cf. Aṅguttara N. I. 25).

Soṇadinnā.

Soṇadinnā, a female devotee living at Nālandā used to serve the bhikkhus with the four requisites and used to observe the precepts and the uposatha with perfect regularity. She meditated on the four noble truths and attained Sotāpatti. (Vimānavatthu Commy. 115).

Uposathā.

Uposathā, a female devotee, living at Sāketa used to offer four requisites to the bhikkhus and meditated on the four noble truths. Thus she attained Sotāpatti. (Vimānavatthu Commy. p. 115).

Alomā.

Alomā, a poor woman living at Sāvatthī in Benares, not finding anything to offer, presented some rotten cooked rice without salt to the Buddha who accepted it. In consequence of this good deed, she, after death, was reborn in the Tavatiṁsa heaven. (Vimānavatthu commentary, p. 184).

Muttā.

Muttā came of a rich brahmin family of Sāvatthī, when she was 20 years old, she went to Mahāpajāpatī the Gotamī and got ordination from her. She practised Kammaṭṭhāna and was instructed by the Buddha to get herself free from all bonds. Afterwards she became an Arahat. (Th. Commy. 8-9).

Puṇṇa.

Puṇṇā was the daughter of a leading burgess of Sāvatthī. When she was about 20 years of age, she heard the Great Pajāpatī teach the doctrine and she renounced the world. She practised insight being encouraged by the Master. In due course she attained Arahatship. (Th. Commy. 9-10).

Dantikā.

Dantikā came of a purohita's family at Kośala. When she came of age, she acquired faith in the Buddha in the Jetavana and later entered the Order under Mahāpajāpatī Gotamī at Rājagaha. While staying at

Rājagaha, she climbed the Vulture's peak after her meal and while resting she developed insight and soon obtained Arahatship with analytical knowledge. (Th. Commy. pp. 51-52).

Vaḍḍhesī. Vaḍḍhesī was the nurse of Mahāpajāpatī Gotamī when her mistress renounced the world, she followed her. For twenty-five years she was harassed by the lusts of the senses and failed to acquire concentration of mind. One day she heard Dhammadinnā preach the Norm. She then began to practise meditation. Very soon she acquired the six supernatural powers. (Th. Commy. 75-76).

Uttama. Uttamā came of a householder's family at Bandhumati. When she grew old, she heard Paṭācārā preach and entered the Order. When Paṭācārā gave her admonition, she was established in insight and very soon won Arahatship. (Th. Commy. pp. 47-48). Thirty sisters born in different families of different places heard Paṭācārā preach and were converted by her and entered the Order. They practised insight and in course of time they won Arahatship with paṭisambhidā. (Th. Commy. pp. 118-120).

Uttarā. Uttarā came of a certain clansman's family at Sāvatthī. When grown up she heard Paṭācārā preach the Norm. She became a believer, entered the Order and became an Arahant. (Th. Commy. pp. 161-162).

Uttarī. Uttarī was a therī who was 120 years old. She went to beg for alms. Once while going for alms she met the Buddha on the way and when going to salute him, she fell down. The Buddha delivered a sermon to her and she having obtained the first stage of sanctification died. (D. C. Vol. III. p. 110).

Khujjuttarā. Khujjuttarā was the maid-servant of Sāmāvatī, queen of King Udena of Kosambī. Her daily duty was to buy flowers from Sumana, a garland-maker for eight kahāpanas. Once the Buddha together with the bhikkhusaṁgha was invited to take meals in Sumana's house. Khajjuttarā waited on her and heard the sermon delivered by the Buddha. She obtained Sotāpattiphalam after hearing the sermon. In former days she used to steal four kahāpanas out of eight kahāpanas given to her by her mistress for buying flowers. After having obtained Sotāpattiphalam she brought flowers to the value of eight kahāpanas. She confessed her guilt when asked why she brought such a large quantity of flowers. She told Sāmāvatī that she had acquired knowledge and came to realise that stealing things is a sin committed by a person who listened to the Buddha's sermon. Sāmāvatī after listening to the dhamma repeated by her obtained Sotāpattiphalam. She was well-versed in Tripiṭaka (D. C. I., pp. 208 ff).

Dinnā. Dinnā was an upāsikā of the Buddha. She was the queen of the King Uggasena. A king promised to the deity of a nigrodha tree that he would worship the deity with blood of one hundred kings of Jambudīpa if he got the throne after his father's death. He then defeated all the kings gradually and went to worship the deity but the deity seeing that many kings would be killed, being compassionate to them, refused his worship on the ground that the queen of King Uggasena whom he defeated was not brought. The king had her brought and she preached a sermon on the avoidance of life-slaughter in their presence. The deity approved and the king refrained himself from life-slaughter, and released the defeated and captured kings who praised Dinnā for her act. It was due to her that so many kings were saved. (D. C. II. pp. 15 foll.)

Sonā.

Sonā came of a clansman's family at Sāvatthī. In course of time, after marriage, she became the mother of ten sons and was known as Bahuputrika. The Dhammapada commentary says that she had seven sons and seven daughters (D. C. II. pp. 276-278). On her husband's renouncing the world, she divided all her riches equally among her sons. In a very short time her sons and daughters-in-law ceased to show her respect. She then entered the Order of the bhikkhuṇīs and began to practise insight strenuously in her old age. The Master gave her suitable instructions. Sonā bhikkhuṇī then attained Arahatship. (Th. Commy. 95). She occupied the foremost place among the bhikkhuṇīs making great exertions (Manorathapūraṇī 218-219; cf. A. N. I. 25).

Bhaddā Kundalakesā.

Bhaddā Kuṇḍalakesā came of the family of a banker at Rājagaha. When grown up, she one day saw Satthuka the purohita's son being led to execution by the city guard. She fell in love with him at first sight. She resolved to die if she did not get him. Her father heard of this and got Satthuka released by bribing the guard heavily. Satthuka was brought to Bhaddā who decked in jewels waited upon him. He saw her jewels and coveted them. He told Bhaddā to get ready an offering to be given to the cliff deity. Bhaddā did so. She adorned herself with all her jewels and accompanied her husband to the precipice with an offering. On reaching the top of the precipice, Satthuka told her to put off all her ornaments which he had come there to take. In vain Bhaddā pleaded that she herself and all her ornaments belonged to him. Satthuka did not take any care of her pleadings. He wanted all her ornaments. Bhaddā then prayed for an embrace with all her jewells on. Satthuka granted her prayer. Bhaddā embraced him in front and then as if embracing him from the back pushed him over the precipice. Satthuka died. (Cf. Dhammapada Commy., Vol. II. pp. 217 foll). Thereafter Bhaddā did not come home but she left the world and entered the Order of the Nigaṇṭhas. She learnt the doctrine of the Nigaṇṭhas and left their company. Thereafter she found no one equal to debate with her. She set up the branch of a Jambu tree on a heap of sand at the gate of some village or town with the declaration that any body able to join issue with her in debate should trample this bough. Sāriputta ordered some children who were near the bough, to trample it. The children did so When Bhaddā saw the bough trampled, she challenged Sāriputta to a debate before some Śākyan recluses as witnesses. But she was defeated and was advised to go to the Buddha for refuge. She went to the Buddha who discerned the maturity of her knowledge. Buddha spoke a verse and she attained Arahatship with analytical knowledge. (Th. Commy. pp. 99 foll). Bhaddā was assigned a chief place among the bhikkhuṇīs possessing ready wit. (Manorathapūraṇī; p. 375; Cf. Aṅguttara Nikāya I. 25).

Sāmā. Sāmā came of a rich householder at Kosambī. She was moved by the death of her dear friend, the lay disciple Sāmāvatī. One day she listened to Elder Ānanda preaching and acquired insight. On the seventh day after this she attained Arahatship with thorough grasp of the Dhamma in form and meaning (Th. Commy. 44-45).

Another Sāmā. Another Sāmā who came of a clansman's family at Kosambī, was a friend of Sāmāvatī whose death afflicted her so much that she could not gain self-control for 25 years. In her old age she heard a sermon through which her insight expanded and she won Arahatship with paṭisambhidā (analytical knowledge) (Th. Commy. 45-46).

Ubbirī. Ubbirī came of the family of a rich householder at Sāvatthī. She was very beautiful and was brought to the palace by the king of Kosala. A few years after a daughter was born to her. This daughter was named Jivā. The king saw the child and was very much pleased. He then had Ubbirī anointed as queen. After a few years Jivā died. The mother used to go to the cemetery and shed tears. Questioned by the Exalted One as to why she was weeping, she said that she was shedding tears for her deceased daughter. She was questioned by the Exalted One as to for which of the 84,000 daughters she was weeping. She then spent a little thought and intelligence over the Norm thus taught by the Buddha. She was established in insight and in due course she won Arahatship by virtue of great merits. (Therīgāthā Commy. 53-54).

Kisāgotamī.

Kisāgotamī came of a poor family at Sāvatthī. She was married to a rich banker's son who had 40 koṭis of wealth. (D. C. II. pp. 270-275). Bodhisattva was her maternal uncle's son. One day while the Bodhisattva was returning home after receiving the news of Rāhula's birth, he was seen by Kisāgotamī from her palace. Buddha's beauty pleased Kisāgotamī so much that she uttered a stanza, the purport of which is, "the mother who has such a child and the father who has such a son and the wife who has such a husband are surely happy (nibbuta) but the Bodhisattva took the word nibbuta in the sense of nibbāṇam." The Bodhisattva presented her with a pearl necklace for making him hear such an auspicious and sacred word. (D. C. Vol. I p. 85; Cf. Atthasālinī, p. 34). On the death of her only child she went to the Buddha with the dead body and requested him to bring the dead to life. Buddha asked her to bring a little mustard seed from a house where not a man died. Kisāgotamī turned from house to house but she came back to Buddha quite unsuccessful. The Buddha delivered a sermon which led her to become a bhikkhuṇī. Her insight grew within a short time and she attained Arahatship.

(Therīgāthā commy. 174). Then the Master assigned her the foremost place among the bhikkhuṇīs who used very rough and simple robe (A N. I. p. 25; cf. Manorathapūraṇī, p. 380). Once Kisāgotamī went to Andhavana to meditate. Māra came to her and told her "You have killed your sons and now you are crying here. Why are you not searching for another man?" Kisāgotamī replied, "I have completely destroyed my sons and my husbands and I have no sorrow. I am not afraid of you, my attachment is destroyed and ignorance is dispelled. Killing the army of death I live sinless." Māra then left her (S. N. I. pp, 129-130). Once Kisāgotamī was coming through the sky to worship the Buddha while Sakka with his retinue was seated before the Buddha. She did not come to the Buddha but worshipped him from the sky and went away. Being questioned by Sakka, the Buddha answered that she was his daughter, Kisāgotamī who was foremost among the bhikkhuṇīs who used very rough and simple robes. (D. C. IV. 156-157).

Paṭācārā.

Paṭācārā came of a banker's family at Sāvatthī. In her youth she formed an intimacy with a servant of her house. On the day fixed for her marriage with another youth of equal rank she eloped with her lover and dwelt in a hamlet. There she used to perform household duties and her lover used to bring wood from forest and work in the field belonging to others. Shortly afterwards Paṭācārā gave birth to a child but at the time of the birth of her second child, a storm arose. Her husband went to forest to cut grass and sticks. While he cut a stake from a tree standing in an ant-hill, a snake came from the ant-hill and bit him. He fell there and died. The next morning Paṭācārā went to the forest with her two children and found her husband dead. She lamented and left the place. On her way to her father's house there was a river the water of which was knee-deep. She lost her children while crossing the river. With tears of grief she came to Sāvatthī and learnt that her parents and brother had perished under the debris of the fallen house. She turned mad. Since then she did not wear cloth and was therefore known as Paṭācārā. One day the Exalted One saw her in that plight and said, "Sister! Recover your shamelessness." She regained her conscience and the Lord taught her that sons, parents and kinsfolk were no shelter and asked her to discern this truth in order to quickly make clear the way to Nibbāṇa. Then she was established in the sotāpattiphalam. The Buddha gave her suitable instructions. She attained Arahatship with analytical knowledge. (Th. Commy. p. 108 foll; Manorathapūraṇī, pp. 356-360; cf. A. N. I. 25). Thereafter she preached the Buddha's dhamma and converted many afflicted women into Buddhist faith. The Therīgāthā Commy. says that Paṭācārā had five hundred female disciples who came of different families of different places. They were married, bore children and lived domestic lives. Overwhelmed with grief at the loss of children they went to Paṭācārā who asked them not to weep when the manner of birth and death was unknown to them. They were greatly moved by Paṭācārā's teachings and renounced the world under her. They performed exercises for insight and soon became established in Arahatship with patisambhidā. (Th.

commy. pp. 122-123; Cf. Dhammapada Commentary, II, p. 260 foll).

Vasiṭṭhi.

Vāsiṭṭhī came of a clansman's family at Vaiśālī. Her parents gave her in marriage to a clansman's son of equal position. She had a son. When the child was able to run about he died. Vāsiṭṭhī was mad with grief. She came to Mithilā and there she saw the Exalted One, self-controlled and self-contained. At the sight of the Buddha she got back her normal mind from the frenzy that had caught hold of her. The master taught her the outlines of the Norm. Performing all proper duties, she acquired insight and struggling with the help of full knowledge, she soon attained Arahatship together with a thorough grasp of the Norm in form and spirit. (Th. commy. 124-125).

Dhammadinnā.

Dhammadinnā came of a clansman's family at Rājagaha and became the wife of a seṭṭhi named Visākhā. One day her husband heard the master teaching and after hearing it he did not speak nor touch her as he used to do before, and renounced the worldly life. Dhammadinnā too became a bhikkhuṇī and took up her residence in a village. One of the great merits acquired by her in her previous births was her subjugation of the complexities of thought, word and deed. By virtue of this merit, she soon attained Arahatship together with thorough mastery of the form and meaning of the Dhamma. Then she returned to Rājagaha and was questioned by her husband on the Khandhas and the like. She answered these questions so correctly that she was praised by the Buddha and was ranked as the foremost among the Sisters who could preach (Th. commy. 15; Cf. Manorathapūraṇī, pp. 360-363; Aṅguttara N. I. 25).

Dhammā. Dhammā came of a respectable family at Sāvatthī, given in marriage to a suitable husband, she became converted. On her husband's death, she entered the Order. In due course she won Arahatship with thorough knowledge of the Norm in form and meaning. (Th. commy. p. 23).

Mettikā. Mettikā was the daughter of a rich brahmin of Rājagaha. She climbed a hill and lived like a recluse. She acquired insight and within a short time won Arahatship. (Th. Commy. p. 35).

Abhayā. Abhayā came of a respectable family at Ujjain. She was a friend of Abhayamātā. She followed her in renouncing the world, and entered the Order. In course of time she attained Arahatship at Rājagaha (Th. Commy. 41-43).

Somā. Somā was born at Rājagaha as the daughter of the purohita of King Bimbisāra. When advanced in years she became a lay disciple. Afterwards she entered the Order of the bhikkhuṇīs. She performed exercises of insight and within a short time won Arahatship. Māra tried in vain to deviate her from this path. From the Saṁyutta Nikāya we learn that Māra came to her and told her, "what is to be obtained by the rishis, you are with slight wisdom trying to have it. That which is difficult to be obtained by Great sages, you being a silly woman, want to have it." She replied, "If my mind is steadfast, I must acquire it, my womanly nature will not prevent me from acquiring it." Māra then left her. (Th. commy. 66-67; cf. S. N. I. p. 129).

Bhaddā Kapilānī.

Bhaddā Kapilānī came of a brahmin family of the Kosiya clan at Sāgala. She was married to a young noble Pippali at the village of Mahātittha. When her husband renounced the world she made over her wealth to her kinsfolk. She then left the world and dwelt five years in the hermitage of the heretics. Thereafter she was ordained by Mahāpajāpatī Gotamī. Establishing insight she won Arahantship. By the Master she was ranked first among the bhikkhuṇīs who could remember previous births. (Th. commy. 67 foll; Cf. Manorathapūraṇī, p. 375; cf. Aṅguttara N. I. 25).

Besides the women who embraced homeless life and became bhikkhuṇīs and therīs, there were others who were staunch believers in the Buddha's Dhamma. These women used to lead domestic life offering charities in the shape of coin and kind to theras, bhikkhus and bhikkhuṇīs in the expectation of a happier rebirth or to the benefit of departed relations. The incidents in the life of some of these women are recorded in the Buddhist literature and would not be out of place here to mention them below:—

Uttarā, daughter of Nandaka, Commander-in-chief of Piṅgala, King of Suraṭṭha, was a believer in the Buddha. She used to offer to a saintly thera cold and perfumed drink as well as excellent cake and sweets to the benefit of her departed father (Paramatthadīpanī on the Petavatthu, pp. 244-257).

A pious woman built a very beautiful house for the bhikkhusaṁgha and invited the Buddha together with the Bhikkhus. After feeding them there she offered the house to the Saṁgha (P. D. on the Petavatthu, 186-191).

A girl of Sāvatthī was a great believer in the Buddha. Once she welcomed a bhikkhu and offered him a seat. In consequence of this meritorious deed she was reborn in a golden vimāna (Vimāna. Commy. pp. 5-6).

A woman of Sāvatthī most gladly offered a seat covered with a piece of blue cloth to a thera who came to her house. After death she was reborn in a vimāna made up of Veḷuriya (lapis lazuli) (Vimānavatthu commentary, pp. 26-27).

A woman of Rājagaha gladly welcomed an arahat and offered him a piṭha (tool) which the thera took with him and presented to the Saṁgha. The woman after death was born in the golden mansion of the Tāvatiṁsa heaven (Ibid, pp 27-28).

A daughter of a family of Rājagaha saw King Bimbisāra coming out of his palace with a large retinue and a display of royal splendour. She thought within her mind and enquired what merit had qualified the king for the acquisition of so much wealth and power. She learnt from the learned that it was charity only. She invited Sāriputta, made him sit on the decorated seat and offered him the food already prepared for him. She presented the thera with new clothes and couch. In consequence of this meritorious deed she was reborn in the golden mansion in the Tāvatiṁsa Heaven (Vimānavatthu commy. p. 31 foll).

A certain woman noticed a tired and thirsty thera, invited him to her house, offered him a seat and brought him water to wash his legs with, and also oil to rub them with. Shortly afterwards she brought a well-scented cold drink for him. In consequence of this meritorious deed she after death, was reborn in the Tāvatiṁsa heaven (Ibid. p 44).

Lakhumā lived near one of the gates of Benares. She used to offer a spoonful of rice to the bhikkhus when they entered the town by that gate. Thus she acquired the habit of offering charity. In the āsanasālā (rest house) she used to prepare seats and supply water to the bhikkhus. She was established in Sotāpatti. After death she was reborn in the Tāvatiṁsa heaven (Vimānavatthu commy. pp. 97-98).

A daughter of a certain upāsaka of Rājagaha was very much devoted to Mahāmoggallāna. One day she welcomed the Thera, offered him a seat, worshipped him with a garland of sumana flowers and gave him sweets, etc. On her death, she was born in the Tāvatiṁsa heaven (V. C. 178-179).

Mallikā was the daughter of a brahmin steward of the Sākya Mahānāman. On her father's death she was taken by Mahānāman to his house. She was at first named Tchandra. She made a wreath which satisfied Mahānāman so much that he changed her name to Mallikā. One day Mallikā went to the garden with her food and just then the Blessed One passed that way collecting alms. Mallikā thought of offering her food to Buddha and the latter knowing her thought held out his bowl. She put her offering in it and wished at the same time that some day she might be free from slavery or poverty. One day Pasenadi carried away by the horse in the heat of the chase came to Mahānāman's garden. There he saw Mallikā. Requested by the king, Mallikā rubbed his feet with a towel. As soon as she did so the king fell asleep, when he awoke he found out who she was, went to Mahānāman and married her. She was then taken to Śrāvastī and in course of time she brought forth a son named Virudhaka (Rockhill, Life of the Buddha, pp. 75-77) and also a daughter. (S. N., I., p. 86). This story is but a Tibetan version of the story of Pasenadi and Vāsabhakhattiyā.

Again we read that Mallikādevī went to the Buddha and asked him thus, "What is the cause of a woman's getting an ugly appearance, bad habit, wretched state, and poverty in this world? What is the cause of a woman who is of this nature becoming very rich and influential? What is the cause of a woman who is of good appearance and lovely becoming poor and uninfluential and vice versa." The Buddha answered, "The woman who is very hot tempered and who gets angry for slight reason becomes poor and ugly if she does not offer any charity to the samaṇas or brāhmaṇas, but if she offers charity to the samaṇas or brāhmaṇas, she becomes rich and influential although she is hot tempered." The Buddha further said thus, "A woman who is not hot tempered and does not become angry for slight reason becomes poor and uninfluential if she does not offer any charity to the samaṇas or brāhmaṇas." Mallikā admitted that on account of her hot temper and pevish nature she got ugly appearance but on account of her previous charities she became a queen. She further said that she would treat properly the daughters of the Kṣatriyas, the Brāhmaṇas and other householders who were subordinate to her. She became a devotee of the Buddha being very pleased with him. (Aṅguttara Nikāya, II. pp. 202-205).

It is noteworthy that once Mallikā was asked by Pasenadi whether she had anybody dearer to her than her own soul. She replied in the negative. Pasenadi was asked the same question by his wife and he too answered it in the negative. He then went to Buddha and related the matter to him. The Buddha said that they were right in holding that there was nothing more favourite than one's own soul. (Udāna, p. 47 ; cf. also S. N. I. p. 75).

Once Pasenadi invited Buddha to teach dhamma to queens Mallikā and Vāsabhakhattiyā as they were desirous of learning it. Buddha asked the king to engage Ānanda for the purpose as it was not possible for him to go every day. Mallikādevī learnt it thoroughly and Vāsabhakhattiyā was not so mindful of learning dhamma. (D. C. I. 382). It was Mallikā who saved the life of many living beings who were brought for sacrifice to save Pasenadi from evil effect of hearing four horrible sounds at midnight by inducing him to go to the Buddha to receive instructions from him. (D. C., Vol. II. pp. 7-8). After her death Mallikādevī had to suffer in the Avīci hell because she deceived her husband by telling a lie about her misconduct. (D. C. III. 119 foll).

Mallikādevī made the following arrangements on the occasion of Pasenadi's offering unique gift to the Buddha and the Bhikkhus.

(1) She made a canopy with sāla wooden parts under which 500 bhikkhus could sit within the parts and 500 outside them.

(2) 500 white umbrellas were raised by 500 elephants standing at the back of 500 bhikkhus.

(3) Golden boats were placed in the middle of the pandal and each Khattiya daughter threw scents standing in the midst of two bhikkhus.

(4) Each Khattiya princess was found standing in the midst of two bhikkhus.

(5) Golden boats were filled with scents and perfumes. (D. C., III., pp. 184 foll).

The daughter of queen Mallikā was also named Mallikā. She was the wife of General Bandhula. She was childless for a long time. Bandhula sent her to her father's house. On the way she went to the Jetavana to salute the Buddha who was informed by her that her husband was sending her home as she was childless. The Buddha asked her to go to her husband's house. Bandhula was informed of this fact and thought that the Buddha must have got the idea that she would be pregnant. The sign of pregnancy was visible in her and she desired to drink water and bathe in the well-guarded tank of the Licchavis. Bandhula with his wife attacked the tank and made his wife bathe and drink water of the tank. (D. C., I., pp. 349-351). Mallikā, wife of Bandhula and daughter of a Malla king of Kusinārā, offered worship to the relics of the Buddha with a plenty of perfumes and garlands and also an ornamant named Mahālatā which was very valuable. In consequence of this, she, after death, was reborn in the Tāvatiṁsa heaven where she was bedecked in all yellow. (V. C. 165).

Vajirā was a bhikkhuṇī who was tempted by Māra when she went to Andhavana to meditate. Māra came to her and asked her, "who has created the being? wherefrom it has come and whereto will it go?" She said, "The aggregation of five khandhas constitute the sattās." Māra then left her. (Saṁyutta Nikāya I. pp. 134-135).

Cīrā bhikkhuṇī was given a robe by an upāsaka of the Buddha. This message was declared by a Yakkha in the streets of Rājagaha saying that a giver by giving a robe to Cīrā who was free from fetters, could acquire much merit. (Saṁyutta Nikāya, I. p. 213).

Many bhikkhuṇīs went to Mahākassapa and received religious instructions from him. Of them a bhikkhuṇī named Thullatissā abused Mahākassapa's teachings in Ānanda's presence. This fact was brought to the notice of Ānanda who remarked that it was beyond her power to appreciate Mahākassapa's attainments. Thullatissā had to renounce the Order on account of her having abused all the Arahats. (Samyutta Nikāya, II. pp. 215 foll.).

Uttarā and her husband were serving a seṭṭhi at Rājagaha. Once the seṭṭhi went to attend a famous ceremony and Uttarā with her husband was at home. The husband of Uttarā went to cultivate in the morning. Uttarā was going with cooked food to her husband in field. On the way she met Sāriputta who just rose up from nirodhasamāpatti and offered the food to him with the result that she became the richest lady at Rājagaha and her husband became a seṭṭhi named Mahādhanaseṭṭhi. (D. C. III. pp. 302 foll).

Puṇṇā was the maid-servant of a banker of Sāvatthī. Once she was asked to husk a large quantity of paddy. While engaged in husking the paddy at night, she went outside the house to take rest. At this time Dabba, a mallian, was in charge of making arrangements for the sleeping accommodation of the bhikkhus who were guests. Puṇṇā with some cakes went out to enquire of the cause of their movements with lights at night. The Buddha went out for alms on the way in which Puṇṇā was. She offered all the cakes to the Buddha without keeping anything for her. The Buddha accepted them. Puṇṇā was thinking whether Buddha would partake of her food. The Buddha did partake of it in her house. The effect of this offer was that Puṇṇā obtained sotāpattiphalam at the place where the offer was made. (D. C., III., pp. 321 ff).

Rohiṇī was Anuruddha's sister. She was suffering from white leprosy. She did not go to her brother as she was suffering. Anuruddha sent for her and asked her to build a rest-house for bhikkhus to get rid of her sin. She kept the rest-house clean even when it was under construction and she did with great devotion for a long time. She became free from her disease and shortly afterwards the Buddha went to Kapilavatthu and sent for Rohiṇī. The Buddha told her that she was the queen of the king of Benares in her former birth. The king was enamoured of the beauty of a dancing girl. The queen knowing this was jealous of the girl and to punish her she put something in her cloth and bathing water which produced terrible itching all over her body. On account of this sin, she got this disease. She obtained sotāpattiphalam and the colour of her body was golden. (D. C. III. pp. 295 foll).

A cultivator's daughter was in charge of the paddy field. She was frying paddy in the field. At that time Mahākassapa was engaged in meditation for a week in the Pipphali cave. Rising up from meditation he went to the girl for alms. She with a delightful mind offered fried grains to him which he accepted. The girl while returning to the spot where she was frying, was smitten by a poisonous snake and she died instantly. She after death was reborn in the golden mansion of the Tāvatiṁsa heaven on account of this meritorious deed and she was named there as Lājadevadhitā who came from heaven to get more merit by serving Mahākassapa. She used to cleanse his monastery and keep water ready for his use. After two days since, she was forbidden to serve him any more as she was found out to be a devī. She lamented much for not being able to serve him. The Buddha came to know of it and preached a sermon to her with the result that she obtained sotāpattiphalam. (D. C., III., pp. 6-9).

Mother of Kumārakassapa became pregnant before she renounced the worldly life but she did not know it. After she became a bhikkhuṇī it was known that she had become pregnant. The matter was referred to the Buddha who asked Upāli to enquire into the matter. Upāli referred to Pasenadi, Anāthapiṇḍika and Visākhā. Visākhā was afterwards solely entrusted to decide the matter. She decided the matter by finding that she was pregnant before her renouncing the world. (D. C., III., 144 ff).

Suppavāsā Koliyadhitā was pregnant for 7 years but she did not give birth to any child. After seven years, labour pain arose and she suffered for seven days terribly but no child was born. She requested her husband to go to the Buddha and to salute him on her behalf reporting the matter to him. Her husband went to the Buddha and informed him. The Buddha desired that Suppavāsā should give birth to a son without any pain and disease, while the Buddha was expressing this desire, a son was born. Her husband was sent again to invite the Buddha in her house for seven days. The Buddha accepted the invitation. The Master took his meal there for 7 days and converted both of them. (Udāna, pp. 15-17; cf. D. C. IV. 192-193). Suppavāsā used to give alms daily to five hundred bhikkhus. (Dhammapada Commentary. I. 339). She became the foremost of the Upāsikās offering the best food to the Buddha. Buddha told her the good effect of offering food and he further says that an offerer by offering rice offers the lease of life, beauty, happiness and strength. The offerer in return obtains celestial life, celestial beauty, happiness and strength. (Aṅguttara Nikāya, II., pp. 62-63).

There was a bhikkhunī named Jaṭilāgāhiya who went to Ānanda at Sāketa and asked him about the effect of samādhi in which mind is fixed and unshakable. Ānanda replied, "The effect of that samādhi is the attainment of saintship. (A. N. IV. 427-428)

Another bhikkhunī of some repute was Nakulamātā who told her husband who was ill and ready to die being free from anxiety that she knew spinning and weaving and management of household affairs and children. She also told her husband that she would never marry after his death as both of them lived the life of a recluse for 16 years and that after his death she would meet the Buddha and the Bhikkhusaṁgha. She also promised to observe the precepts. She also told her husband that she was one of upāsikās who fully observed the precepts, controlled mind, had strong faith in the Buddha, Dhamma and Saṁgha and who became fearless and not dependent on others except the Buddha for support. (A. N., III. 295 foll).

Bojjhā was a devotee. She approached the Buddha who preached to her the reward of observing the sīla and the uposatha and told her thus, "Happiness obtained by observing uposatha is sixteen times greater than that enjoyed by the sixteen countries. (A. N. IV., 259-260).

Velukaṇṭakī Nandamātā was a devotee of the Buddha. She gave offerings to Sāriputtta and Moggallāna. Referring to this the Buddha said, "A giver must be pleased before he gives dāna, his mind must be pleased while giving dāna and after giving dāna. The receiver of the offering must be free from rāga, dosa and moha. The consequence of such a gift is immeasurable". Nandamātā gave such a gift to Sāriputta and Moggallāna and she obtained immeasurable consequence of the gift. (A. N. III. 336-337).

There was another bhikkhuṇī named Nandamātā who was once repeating the Pārāyaṇa Sutta of the Sutta Nipāta in a sweet voice. King Vessavana was going from north to south and he waited there till Nandamātā finished her repetition and he praised her much. Nandamātā told Vessavana that let the merit acquired by this act be beneficial to him. Vessavana gladly accepted it and told her that the merit which would be acquired by her through the gift made to Sāriputta and Moggallāna would prove beneficial to him. (A. N. IV. p. 63 foll.).

Migasālā was an Upāsikā who went to Ānanda and told him, "According to the instruction of the Buddha, a brahmacārī and an abrahmacārī go to the same place after death and enjoy the same amount of happiness. Ānanda went to the Buddha to have the solution of this problem. The Buddha said that the upāsikā was ignorant and uneducated and therefore she could not realise it properly. The Buddha further said, "Even a householder may acquire the same amount of merit as acquired by a brahmacārī who does not fulfill his duties properly. (A. N. III. 347 foll.).

Dinnā, a bhikkhuṇī, was asked by her husband to explain Sakkāyadiṭṭhi, Sakkāyanirodha, ariyaṭṭhanikamaggo, Saṁkhāra, nirodha-samāpatti, manner of rising up from nirodha-samāpatti and Vedanā. Dhammadinnā gave satisfactory answers to all the questions. She said, "Five upādāna khandhas constitute sakkāya. Tanhā means Sakkāya samudayo. Destruction of Tanhā means Sakkāya nirodha. The noble eight-fold path is the means of attaining Sakkāyanirodha. Ignorant people take the five upādāna Khandhas jointly and separately as attā (soul), the noble disciples do not take them in this sense. Those who obtain nirodha samāpatti are stopped one after another. The three kinds of Vedanā are sukha, dukkha and adukkhamasukha (M. N. I. 299 foll.).

There was an upāsikā named Sujātā who destroyed three samyojanas and obtained sotāpatti. (S. N. V. p. 356).

Nandā was a bhikkhuṇī who was a sister of the king Kosala. While going through the sky at night she instructed Kālāsoka and the bhikkhusaṁgha to purify bhikkhusaṁgha by driving out bad bhikkhus and protecting good bhikkhus. (Sāsanavaṁsa p. 6).

Sāmāvatī was the queen of King Udena of kosambī. The harem containing Sāmāvatī with 500 female attendants was burnt while Udena was in the royal garden. The matter was referred to the Buddha who said, "Each upāsikā had gone according to her kamma, some have become sotāpannā, sakadāgāmī, anāgāmī and so forth (Udāna, p. 79).

Lilāvatī was the chief queen of Parākkamavāhu of Laṅkā. She was very intelligent. She belonged to the family of King Paṇḍu of Ceylon. (Dāṭhāvaṁsa). There was a maid-servant named Bīraṇī engaged by Aśokabrāhmana to give food daily to the saṁgha which was enough for eight bhikkhus. This she used to do with devotion and after her death she was born in a vimāna. (Mahāvaṁsa, p. 214).

Rūpanandā was Buddha's step-sister. She thought that her eldest brother had renounced the world and had become a Buddha. Her younger brother Nandā was a bhikkhu and Rāhulakumāra had obtained ordination and her husband too had become a bhikkhu and her mother Mahāpajāpatī Gotamī a bhikkhuṇī. She renounced the world thinking that so many of her relatives did renounce the world. She did not go before the Buddha as she was proud of her beauty while the Buddha used to preach impermanence and worthlessness of rūpa. The other bhikkhuṇīs and bhikkhus always used to praise the Buddha in her presence and told her that all having different taste had become pleased by seeing the Buddha. (Dhammapada commentary, III., p. 115).

Nandā was the wife of a householder named Nandasena who lived in a certain village near Sāvatthī. She had no faith in the Buddha. She was very hot-tempered and used to abuse her husband, father-in-law, and mother-in-law. On her death she became a petī. One day she appeared before her husband and gave him an account of her past misdeeds. The husband made gifts for her sake to the bhikkhus and Nandā was released from her miseries. (P. D. on the Petavatthu, 89-92). Nandā thought of going to the Buddha with other bhikkhuṇīs but she would not show her to the Buddha. The Buddha came to know that Nandā had come with the bhikkhunīs. The Buddha desired to lower down pride of her beauty by showing bad effect of it. By his miraculous power the Buddha created a most beautiful girl who was engaged in fanning the Buddha. Nandā seeing her beauty, found out that her own beauty was much more inferior. The girl was seen gradually attaining youth, the state of mother of one child and then old age and disease and death. Nandā seeing this gave up pride of her beauty and came to realise impermanence of beauty. The Buddha knowing the state of her mind delivered a suitable sermon and she became an arahat after hearing the sermon. (D. C. III., 113 foll).

Revatī was the daughter of a householder of Benares. She had no faith in the Buddha and was very uncharitable. For some days she was forced by her parents to do meritorious deeds in order to win Nandiya, a neighbour's son, as her husband. After marriage Nandiya caused her to follow him in his meritorious deeds. Thereafter Nandiya had to go abroad. He asked his wife to continue all the meritorious deeds. Revatī did so for seven days. Then she stopped all meritorious deeds and began to abuse the bhikkhus who had come to her house for alms. Nandiya, on his return, found that all his acts or charity had been discontinued. After death Revatī became a petī. On his death Nandiya became a devatā. He saw with his divine eyes that Revatī had become a petī. He then went to her and asked her to approve of the meritorious acts done by him. As soon as she did so, she became a devatā and resided with Nandiya in heaven. (See Vimānavatthu commentary and Suttasaṁgaha).

INDEX